learning disability **today**

learning disability **today**

Key issues for providers, managers, practitioners and users

learning disability today
Key issues for providers, managers, practitioners and users

Edited by Steven Carnaby

© Pavilion/Foundation for People with Learning Disabilities/Tizard Centre

The authors have asserted their rights in accordance with the *Copyright, Designs and Patents Act 1988* to be identified as the authors of this work.

Published by:
Pavilion Publishing (Brighton) Ltd
The Ironworks
Cheapside
Brighton BN1 4GD

Tel: 01273 623222
Fax: 01273 625526
Email: info@pavpub.com
Web: www.pavpub.com

First published 2002.

A Catalogue record for this book is available from the British Library.

ISBN 1 84196 068 3

Pavilion is committed to providing high quality, good value, current training materials and conferences, and bringing new ideas to all those involved in health and social care. Founded by health and social care professionals, Pavilion has maintained its strong links with key agencies in the field, giving us a unique opportunity to help people develop the skills they need through our publications, conferences and training.

The Foundation for People with Learning Disabilities works to improve the lives of people with learning disabilities through research and developing community services.

The Foundation brings together people with learning disabilities, family carers and professionals to plan projects that can then be copied across the UK. In all our work we want to ensure that people with learning disabilities are supported in living as active citizens within the community.

The Foundation for People with Learning Disabilities was established in 1998 as part of the Mental Health Foundation which has been working in both mental health and learning disabilities since 1949.

The Tizard Centre is part of the University of Kent at Canterbury. The Centre is one of the UK's leading academic groups working in learning disability, mental health and services for older people. We provide teaching through short courses, certificate, diploma and postgraduate programmes at the University of Kent and elsewhere, and conduct an extensive programme of research and consultancy.

Pavilion editor: Jo Hathaway
Cover design: Greg Levitt
Page design and layout: Stanford Douglas
Cover illustration: Kevin Chettle
Other illustrations: provided by ActionSpace, Carousel, CHANGE, the Foundation for People with Learning Disabilities (Gold Project), Mencap, roc and David S. Stewart
Printing: Ashford Press (Southampton)

Contents

Contents

Acknowledgements

The production of this book relied on the efforts and support of a wide range of people. First, my thanks to all of the contributing authors for agreeing to participate in this project, some of whom were asked to work to impossibly tight deadlines.

As importantly, my thanks to all those who supplied illustrative material for the book – everyone at ActionSpace; Tilly Gregory at Carousel; Change; Kevin Chettle; the Gold Project at the Foundation for People with Learning Disabilities; Maxine Shannon at Mencap; David O'Driscoll at roc and David Stewart from Shepherd School in Nottingham.

My thanks also go to everybody at Pavilion, the Tizard Centre and the Foundation for People with Learning Disabilities for their advice and guidance at different points of the production process, but in particular Jo Hathaway and Paul Cambridge for their invaluable support throughout.

About the contributors

WORDS

Peter Baker is a consultant clinical psychologist employed by Hastings & Rother NHS Trust (East Sussex County Healthcare NHS Trust from April 2002), and is an honorary lecturer at the Tizard Centre, University of Kent at Canterbury. His professional life has centred on working with people who have learning disabilities and severe challenging behaviour. This has been as a clinician, a teacher of carers and an author.

Alison Brammer is Senior Lecturer in Law at Keele University. Previously, she worked as a solicitor in local government, specialising in social services matters, including childcare, mental health and registered homes tribunals. She is Director of the MA in Childcare Law and Practice at Keele and teaches social work law. She has written numerous articles considering the law relating to vulnerable adults in various settings and has written a legal column in the *Tizard Learning Disability Review*. She currently writes the legal column in the *Journal of Adult Protection*. Her book, *Social Work Law* will be published by Pearson later this year. Alison has been involved in extensive training of social services and health sector personnel.

learning disability **today**

Karen Bunning is a senior lecturer in the Department of Language and Communication Science at City University, providing professional training in speech and language therapy. Her main clinical and research interests lie in promoting communication access and participation for adults with learning disabilities, sensory impairment and the process of intervention.

Paul Cambridge is a senior lecturer at the Tizard Centre. He has recently completed a 12-year evaluation of the outcomes and costs of community care for the Department of Health. His current research interests include the quality of intimate and personal care, physical abuse, gender and sexual identity, men working in social care, care management and joint commissioning. Paul has also published papers and training materials on sexuality and HIV and currently edits the *Tizard Learning Disability Review.*

Steven Carnaby has a background in the direct support of people with learning disabilities. He is currently a clinical psychologist for Parkside NHS Trust working with people with severe and profound learning disabilities, and a lecturer in learning disabilities at the Tizard Centre. His research interests and publications focus on intimate and personal care, individual planning and quality of life issues for people with profound and multiple disabilities. He has published widely in the learning disability field, including co-authoring *Making it Personal* (Pavilion, 2000) and *Designs for Living* (Ashgate, 1999).

Angela Cole is a freelance consultant with more than 20 years' experience working in services for people with learning difficulties. She has worked in a range of settings and roles – from direct support to social work, and lecturing on service management and commissioning. Since going freelance Angela has undertaken review and development work around the country and has been very involved in supporting the implementation of person-centred planning in a number of services. Angela is active in her local community alongside people with learning difficulties as well as in her work.

Margaret Flynn is a senior lecturer at St George's Hospital Medical School and an assistant director of the National Development Team. A former Prince of Wales Fellow with the Royal College of General Practitioners, Margaret has worked with the Department of Health in the drafting of health policy and guidance and has worked with colleagues from the Institute of Medicine, Law and Bioethics in a study of health care decision-making. She is currently doing research with Salomons entitled *An ordinary death?*, and has recently co-authored a book for children with her brother Peter, entitled *Having a Learning Disability*, which is published by Belitha Press.

Nicola Grove was an English teacher before training as a speech and language therapist. She now lectures in the Department of Language and Communication Science at City University, specialising in learning disability, education and augmentative and alternative communication. She provides training and consultancy in communication in severe and profound learning difficulty, storytelling, the use of literature across the range of ability, and the development of the National Curriculum for special educational needs.

Geraldine Holt currently works as a consultant psychiatrist with people with learning disabilities in a community-based service in South East London. Her particular interest is in staff training on the mental health needs of people with learning disabilities. She has written extensively in the field, including co-authoring *Mental Health in Learning Disabilities*, published by Pavilion.

Sheila Hollins is a Fellow of the Royal College of Psychiatrists, a Professor of Psychiatry of Learning Disability at St George's Hospital Medical School and a consultant psychiatrist in South West London. She is seconded to the Department of Health, part time, as a senior policy advisor in learning disability. Her responsibilities include teaching medical students about learning disability and training postgraduate health and social care practitioners, as well as working clinically with adults with learning disabilities. Sheila is a former GP. Her son has a learning disability.

Frank Keating is a lecturer in mental health at the Tizard Centre where he takes a lead in teaching on 'race' and mental health. He has worked in both learning disability and mental health services. Frank is also Chair of the Transcultural Psychiatry Society (UK) and is an advisor to National Mind.

Ann Lloyd is a commissioning manager with the London Borough of Newham. She has worked in community-based services, promoting inclusion for people with learning difficulties. As a job trainer with A Chance to Work, she supported men and women with severe learning difficulties and complex needs into real jobs. She has worked as a staff development officer helping staff gain the skills needed to support the moving-on process during the closure of a hospital for people with learning difficulties. In 1995 she led a team in setting up Hackney Community Resource Service – a community-based team supporting people to realise ordinary goals.

Henrik Lynggaard is Principal Clinical Psychologist at Islington Learning Disabilities Partnership and is involved in teaching and supervision on the Clinical Psychology Doctorate courses at University College London and University of East London. He has a particular interest in ensuring that a broad range of therapeutic modalities are made available to people with learning disabilities.

Michelle McCarthy is a senior lecturer in learning disability at the Tizard Centre, University of Kent. She has worked in the sexuality and learning disability field for many years and has a particular interest in working with women. She has written widely about her work in the professional and academic press.

Annette McDonald has 20 years' experience in direct service provision for a wide range of client groups in differing settings and roles. This had led to a specific interest in people whose needs involve input from more than one service specialism. She has been very involved in the development of self-advocacy for people with learning disabilities, and has been instrumental in the setting up of a successful independent advocacy organisation that is currently monitoring quality of residential service provision. She has recently been researching the needs of older people who have dementia, and her recently published training resource, *Staying Home Alone* (Pavilion, 2001) is aimed at home care providers who support older people with dementia to continue to live in the community. Annette currently works as a freelance trainer and consultant. She has an MA in the Management of Community Care from the Tizard Centre.

Peter McGill is the Director of the Tizard Centre. He has a wide range of previous experience including working in day services, managing residential support to a house for people who previously lived in an institution, and working as a clinical psychologist.

Hazel Morgan joined the Mental Health Foundation in 1996 as Learning Disabilities Manager. Her recent work has included the management of the Choice Initiative, exploring how people with high support needs can bring changes to their lives. Since April 2001 she has been Head of the Foundation for People with Learning Disabilities, set up in 1998 as a part of the Mental Health Foundation. Previously, she was a lecturer in further and higher education. Her younger son, Peter, had severe learning disabilities. In his lifetime she wrote a number of articles from the perspective of a family carer and a book, *Through Peter's Eyes*.

Zenobia Nadirshaw is Consultant Clinical Psychologist and Joint Head of Psychology, Parkside NHS Trust. She has a wide range of experience of teaching, training and research in mental health, learning disabilities and women's issues. Within local and national professional organisations, she has drawn attention to issues of 'race', difference and diversity. Zenobia is a former chair of the Transcultural Psychiatry Society and British Psychological Society award winner for challenging inequality of opportunity.

Wendy Perez is a service user with a learning disability who, for the last five years, has been employed in the Department of Psychiatry of Disability as a training adviser. Having previously worked for People First in London, Wendy has a keen interest in developing accessible materials and contributes to the design and drafting of the Royal College of Psychiatrists and St. George's Hospital Medical School's *Books Beyond Words* series. She teaches on a Diploma Course with Health Care Sciences and on a communication module for undergraduate medical students. Wendy offers consultancy to researchers to develop their capacity to work with consumers as equal partners. She has extensive experience of working with service users and challenging exclusion from decision-making at all levels, and is a member of the Institute for Applied Health and Social Policy Project Team.

Jennie Williams is a clinical psychologist and senior lecturer in mental health at the Tizard Centre. She is primarily interested in the effects of social inequalities on mental health and service provision, but retains a lively interest in the implications of social inequalities for other client groups.

PICTURES

ACTIONSPACE

ActionSpace is one of the largest providers of visual arts projects for people with learning disabilities in Greater London. Our aim is to create opportunities for self-expression, education, training and confidence-building. We work with people of all ages with mild to profound learning disabilities and aim to encourage their integration into the community by running projects in arts venues. All our projects are free of charge to participants and support with transport is provided where necessary. We actively seek to employ people with disabilities and currently have two learning disabled members on our administrative team. We are revenue funded by London Arts and have project grants from several boroughs.

For more information about ActionSpace and to join one of our projects you can call us on 020 7209 4289 or email us at office@actionspace.org; or visit our website at **www.actionspace.org**

ADVOCACY IN ACTION

Advocacy in Action are people of difference who co-work to promote the rights, interests and needs of any person or group on the community's edge who do not get their fair share of respect, resources or opportunity. They are proud to celebrate 12 years of challenging behaviour as an internationally acclaimed training and development team, working to empower people on the receiving end of social care and concern, and those workers who wish to serve them by promoting equitable, respectful and constructive provision.

Kevin Chettle is a survivor of the old institutional life that was enforced on people with learning disabilities for so long. His picture, which has been used for the cover of this book, is one of many he has done which express the experience he had of that institutional life, and celebrate his 'release'.

Now 22 years free from that system, Kevin works as an advocate and trainer. He has committed himself to working with other people with less opportunity than himself, to try to ensure they are supported to access the services and attention they need, to live the full life in the community to which they are entitled. Kevin is a co-director of, and trainer for, Advocacy in Action.

CAROUSEL

Carousel's mission is to provide opportunities for people with learning difficulties to engage with the arts as artists, participants and audience members. By using the arts, Carousel opens up the processes of exploration and discovery, which support individuals in developing skills and confidence. Carousel will also provide further training opportunities for artists with learning difficulties and help bring their work to the attention of the wider arts world and the public at large. Carousel will promote the artwork of people with learning difficulties to challenge perceptions of what 'art' is and who can create it. Carousel is funded by, among others, the Arts Council of England, Brighton & Hove City Council, South East Arts and West Sussex County Council.

High Spin is an integrated dance theatre company of performers with and without learning difficulties, funded by Carousel. Photographs included in this book are taken from the touring shows *Rice Rain* and the *Surgeon's Waltz*.

For more information about Carousel and its projects, and to join one of our projects you can call us on 01273 234734 or email us at carouselcharity@hotmail.com or visit our website at **www.carousel.org.uk**

roc

David O'Driscoll is a psychotherapist working for the roc loss and bereavement service, which is part of Hertfordshire Partnership Trust. The service provides training, support and psychotherapy to learning disabled professionals and service users. He is a founder member of the (IPD) Institute of Psychotherapy and Disability. His other interest is learning disability history, and he is currently researching the history of psychotherapy with people with a learning disability and working on a website, www.learningdisabilityhistory.com, focusing on the history of three main Hertfordshire hospitals.

www.learningdisabilityhistory.com

The website will focus on the three main Hertfordshire Hospitals for people with learning disabilities: Cell Barnes, Leavesden and Harperbury. The information available on the website will consist of the history of each hospital, and reminiscences of their experiences from staff and former service users. There will also be photos, including ones of the hospitals and some of the main events in their history. There will be also practical information on further resources, including how ex-service users can gain access to their medical records. All the information can be downloaded from the website. It will be accessible to people with a learning disability.

www.intellectualdisability.info

This website focuses on the health of people with learning disabilities. It is managed by the Down's Syndrome Association and the Department of Psychiatry at St. George's Hospital Medical School. It is aimed at health professionals and health professionals in training.

CHANGE

CHANGE works and campaigns for people with learning disabilities, and people with learning disabilities who are blind or deaf, to have equal rights in the UK. In CHANGE, learning disabled people and disabled people work together to campaign for accessible information, the right to good services and equality of opportunity. CHANGE uses easy words, pictures and photographs. CHANGE believes in making information easy to understand. CHANGE uses acting, role-play and Forum Theatre.

CHANGE uses a range of communication to suit the needs of individual people who have a learning disability and/or a sensory impairment.

The black and white cartoon illustrations in this book have all been taken from CHANGE's picture bank. For more information about CHANGE and its projects, call us on 020 7639 4312 or 0113 243 0202. We have offices in London and Leeds. You can email us at londonoffice@changepeople.co.uk or change.north@tesco.net.

MENCAP

Mencap is the UK's leading charity working with people with a learning disability and their families and carers.

Mencap campaigns to ensure that people with a learning disability have their rights recognised and are respected as individuals. It also provides services enabling them to live a more independent life as well as giving support to their families and carers. These include residential, education and employment services, leisure opportunities and individual support and advice.

David S. Stewart is Head of Shepherd School in Nottingham, a large day school for students with severe and profound learning disabilities. As a historian, David has a particular interest in the history of learning disabilities. He has provided photographs of life at the Darenth Training Colleges at the turn of the 19–20th century.

 # Foreword by Hilary Brown

Whether you are new to learning disability services or taking time to think about and review your practice, this book will be invaluable to you in your work and as you approach your training within the LDAF framework. For many years learning disability services were known as the 'cinderella' services; users and the staff who served them were both devalued and 'left out'. This text and the training framework which it supports are hopefully the last nail in the coffin of this outdated attitude.

The book is divided into three sections, each with a different focus. The first looks at the context and ethos of the services you work in. It will allow you to think about your values and assumptions, your own experiences of being respected or treated badly and the extent to which people with learning disabilities are marginalised and discriminated against.

The second section is about skills. It is easy to imagine support as something uncomplicated that everyone can do but as you read on you will see how difficult the job you do really is.

The last section of the book zooms in on those areas of practice which are particularly complex: issues where you need additional knowledge to help you understand what is important and to make judgements about what is best. These are the areas of the work where it is not enough to be 'nice', you have to know why you are doing what you are doing for it to make sense and for you to make balanced judgements.

It is not that these ideas are all new or that you will not already bring expertise and understanding to your work. In the past, training initiatives tended to look at one aspect on its own – at values, skills or understanding of special circumstances – but not at all three and at how they interact.

Studying the ideas and approaches outlined in the book will allow you to reassess your values, consolidate your skills and gain new insights into the needs of people with learning disabilities. You may also use the book to underpin your studies as you work towards the new Certificate (LDAF 2) and Advanced Certificate (LDAF 3) in Working With People Who Have Learning Disabilities and as part of the process of accreditation which will help you to get proper acknowledgement for your commitment and expertise.

Hilary Brown
Canterbury Christ Church University College
November 2001

# Introduction

'Improving the lives of people with learning disabilities requires commitment, nationally and locally, to strong principles, a firm value base and clear objectives for services.'

Valuing People: A New Strategy for Learning Disability for the 21st Century
(Department of Health, 2001)

This statement gives a clear message to everybody involved in learning disability services, and underpins an important agenda that emphasises rights, independence, choice and inclusion for every individual. The partnership team of people with learning disabilities, their families and carers, and the services available to support them, certainly has the potential to work towards and achieve this goal.

However, effective partnership also relies on commitment. Sharing ideas and evidence of good practice leads to discussion, which encourages review of approaches that are *assumed* to be meeting needs. Similarly, person-centred support means just that – starting with the person, and remaining alongside them throughout, ensuring involvement and inclusion in every way.

This book offers a framework for fostering such commitment.

The issues raised are divided into three main areas.

The first, **Context and Ethos**, provides historical background as well as a discussion of the values, ideology and legislation underpinning current learning disability provision. Being more aware of our own position in society and what we personally bring to the service setting is essential to good practice, and such awareness is likely to enhance the collaboration between supporters and those being supported. This understanding of context is linked to an understanding of our role and accompanying responsibilities within vital areas such as adult protection. Similarly, acknowledgement of the issues relating to the vulnerability of people with learning disabilities within risk management helps to ensure that we support autonomy and individual expression, and avoid the development of oppressive practices.

The second section of the book sets out a number of **Key Skills** in supporting people with learning disabilities. Each chapter makes suggestions for good practice, from those working in, and in many cases, leading their respective fields, providing ways for the reader to translate into practical strategies the ideology laid out in the first section, to put ideas to work. This selection of chapters emphasises the importance of social inclusion, often illustrated by examples from the authors' own experiences.

The final section focuses on a range of **Key Areas** that often need particular consideration. Again, the authors provide ideas and strategies for addressing some of the difficulties that may arise in supporting people with complex needs, or for ensuring healthy transition and ageing. Throughout, the emphasis is on developing inclusive practices that are built upon the values and principles established in earlier chapters of the book.

This text is intended as an introduction to some of the issues central to the lives of people with learning disabilities and their supporters today. Readers wanting more in-depth coverage are guided towards further reading at the end of each chapter.

The book can also be used as background reading for those studying for the Certificate (LDAF 2), and Advanced Certificate (LDAF 3), in Working With People Who Have Learning Disabilities. It will also provide underpinning knowledge for S/NVQs in Care. It gives context to specific units, and some chapters have been recommended to course participants as core text.

The quotation from *Valuing People* continues…

*'Each individual should have the support and
opportunity to be the person he or she wants to be'.*

It is hoped that *Learning Disability Today* will help readers work towards what is surely the fundamental goal for everybody.

Steven Carnaby

 Part One

CONTEXT AND ETHOS

WRITTEN BY
Steven Carnaby

Chapter 1

THE BIGGER PICTURE

KEY WORDS

acquired

consensus

impairment

lucidity

psychometric
assessment

significant

social functioning

containment

block treatment

*Understanding approaches
to learning disability*

People with learning disabilities form one of the most vulnerable groups in society. Individuals vary significantly in the degree and nature of their disabilities. This variation in the kind of disability people have, and how extreme it is, means that we need to support people to lead their daily lives in a variety of ways, designed to meet their specific needs.

As an introduction to the important issues raised in the reader, this chapter first summarises current thinking about the term 'learning disabilities', looking at its definition and how scientific knowledge continues to establish how it comes about. Secondly, we look at how people with learning disabilities have been perceived through history, culminating in current thinking about 'good support'.

What is 'learning disability'? According to the Department of Health (1998), a diagnosis of learning disability is given when an individual meets three important criteria, in that they have:

- a significant impairment of **intelligence**, as well as
- a significant impairment of **social functioning**, and that
- both of these impairments were **acquired** *before* **adulthood**.

● **Level of intelligence**

A person's 'level of intelligence' is determined by a psychometric assessment (usually administered by a clinical psychologist). This gives a numerical measure of intelligence (an IQ score). A 'significant impairment' is indicated by an IQ score of below 70 (the average for the general population is 100). The lower the IQ, the higher the level of the person's disability/the more their learning is disabled.

● **Social functioning**

'Social functioning' means the individual's ability to cope on a day-to-day basis with their own lives. This includes skills in communication, self-care, home living, social relationships, using community resources (eg shops and cafés), work, leisure, health and safety.

Having a '**significant impairment**' in social functioning suggests that the individual needs significant help to ensure they survive and/or to adapt to daily living.

● **Acquired before adulthood**

'Acquired before adulthood' means that the impairment was acquired before the age of 18 years. In practice, most learning disabilities are present at birth or have an onset in early childhood.

What causes learning disability? The causes of learning disability are divided into three categories:

1 those occurring *before* the child is born (**prenatal causes**)

2 those occurring *during* birth itself (**perinatal causes**)

3 those occurring *after* birth (**postnatal causes**).

Table 1 (below) gives examples of those categories of causes, and descriptions of them.

Table 1: Causes of learning disability

Cause	Syndromes	Examples
Prenatal causes	Genetic syndromes	eg Down's syndrome; Fragile X Syndrome
	Other syndromes	eg spina bifida; cerebral palsy
	Environmental factors	eg malnutrition; drugs; alcohol; diseases
Perinatal causes	Biomedical factors	eg infections in the womb (such as toxoplasmosis)
	Environmental factors	eg asphyxia; premature birth; other difficulties during labour/delivery
Postnatal causes	Biomedical factors	eg epilepsy; meningitis; Rett's syndrome
	Environmental factors	eg head injury; lead/mercury poisoning; malnutrition; social deprivation

The causes listed in **Table 1** prevent the brain from developing in the normal way, which in turn causes problems with thinking and learning. There may also be other problems eg physical disability, sensory impairments, epilepsy and so on.

Values and attitudes towards people with learning disabilities

The way that society sees people with learning disabilities has changed over time. It is important to think about the values that underpin these changes, as these same values also inform the services that support people with learning disabilities and influence how you as a worker provide support. **Figure 1** shows a way of understanding how these influences work.

- **People** (carers) supporting the individual 'interpret' and assess what that individual needs in the way of care.

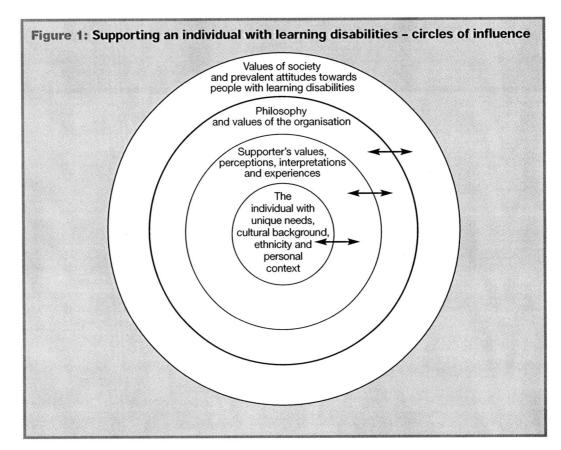

Figure 1: Supporting an individual with learning disabilities – circles of influence

Values of society and prevalent attitudes towards people with learning disabilities

Philosophy and values of the organisation

Supporter's values, perceptions, interpretations and experiences

The individual with unique needs, cultural background, ethnicity and personal context

- The ways in which this process happens are likely to be influenced by the values of the **organisation** that employs the staff member.

- In turn, the organisation designs services in ways that reflect the wider values in **society**.

These '**circles of influence**' are dynamic, in that each layer/circle of support influences and is influenced by the others.

The values inherent within each of the 'circles of influence' are fluid, in that there is not a 'right' way of providing support to vulnerable people. What qualifies as 'good support' is agreed upon and arrived at by consensus. Increasingly, services use the evidence from research studies to inform how they work, and to establish principles of good support that underpin their practices. This scientific approach is relatively new; the following review of how people with learning disabilities have been supported in the past shows how values and attitudes have changed, and the importance of understanding the power of **societal values** in providing health and social care.

A brief history of service provision for people with learning disabilities

Language: idiots and lunatics

Changes in approaches to people with learning disabilities can be charted by tracing changes in the language used to describe them. From medieval times through to the late 19th century, the legal system distinguished between 'lunacy' and 'idiocy'.

The term 'lunacy' referred to individuals with mental health problems (ie people with problematic behaviour that was acquired, who had periods of 'lucidity', and were then well).

'Idiocy' was used to describe individuals with learning disabilities, recognised as an irreversible state originating at birth. 'Idiots' were supported by family members receiving Poor Law relief, or by 'keepers' who provided lodgings and care.

Asylums and workhouses: safety, education and understanding?

The Victorian era saw a significant change. Asylums were created with the aim of educating people with learning disabilities and realising their potential. However, the number of people identified as needing this kind of service was greatly underestimated, and the asylums soon became overcrowded. The solution was to house people with learning disabilities in workhouses and along-side people with mental health problems. Medical professionals began taking over, and emphasis was placed on diagnosis and classification rather than on social care and education.

The advent of industrial society saw further change and increasing hostility towards people with learning disabilities. Work became the centre of daily life, and the drive towards maximising production made no provision for slower individuals who needed more support to achieve the same outcomes as their peers. Everyday living was harsh, and those who could not keep up were despised. Those in power became concerned about people with learning disabilities having children of their own, advocating sterilisation and the repression of sexuality – reflecting values observed in wider society at that time. Institutional care therefore served as a means of containing people who were seen as worthless and unable to contribute to society, and segregated this group from the rest of 'productive' society.

From institution to community living

The first half of the twentieth century saw some changes in legislation, but little changed in the way of provision. In many ways, people with learning disabilities – or 'the mentally handicapped' – were largely forgotten. However, the post-war period saw the development of the NHS and other landmarks reform such as the *Children Act 1948*, which argued that children living in children's homes should be given the opportunity of experiencing a normal life. For many, this is the root of the move towards 'ordinary' living for those individuals subjected to a segregated, institutionalised lifestyle.

The 1971 white paper, *Better Services for the Mentally Handicapped* established the idea of moving people with learning disabilities back into the community. This approach gained pace with the discovery of several scandals in the institutions, which revealed the extent of the poor living conditions and harsh, block treatment that people with learning disabilities had endured, largely unnoticed.

However, it was not until the 1980s and the *Community Care Act 1990* that a clear pathway for making provision in the community was outlined, and the major task of closing the mental handicap hospitals began in earnest. The development of community services has relied on a number of key ideas, described below.

Key ideas   **Normalisation**

Understanding normalisation
The majority of services supporting people with learning disabilities in Britain are heavily influenced by 'normalisation'. Care plans, operational policies, training in good practice – everything to do with quality provision has normalisation at its foundation. But what is 'normalisation'?

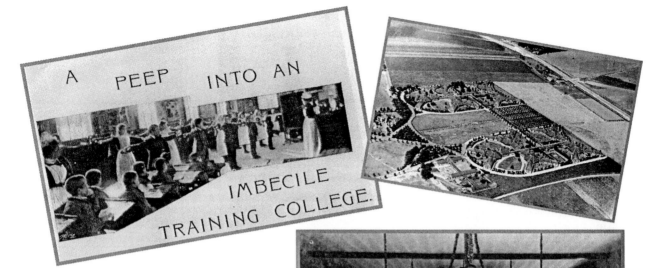

The pictures on this page are taken from a private collection of **'Darenth Colony'**, and give a fascinating look at institutional life and attitudes at the turn of the 20th century.

Top left: Drill at the Darenth Schools, 1898. This article appeared in the first volume of the *Royal Magazine*.

Top right: The Pavilion wards at Darenth, opened in the 1890s as an extension to the main asylum. Notice how remote the site is.

Right: Lines of cots in the children's ward at Darenth School, 1898.

Left and above: People were made to work long hours doing manual jobs such as weaving, repairing shoes and making baskets.

"A good deal of floor space is necessary in a basket shop, otherwise there would be no room for fixing the side stakes in the slarth, or bottom of the basket." (From A. Bickmore, *Industries for the Feeble-minded and Imbecile: A handbook for teachers.*)

These pictures are taken from a selection provided by roc and catalogue life at **Harperbury Hospital** around the middle of the 20th century. Some photos are taken from a 'mental nurse' exhibition. Attitudes had changed to a certain extent, but men and women were still 'kept' separately; they slept in wards and were still thought of as 'patients'.

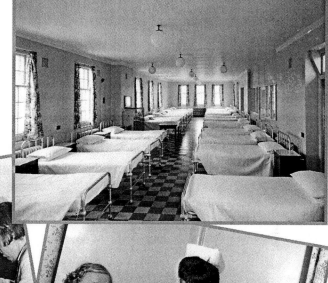

During the day, men still worked in the fields and gardens and did upholstery and basket weaving. Women worked in the kitchens, or were otherwise cleaning, weaving and sewing. Staff members wore uniform. The residents were not free to come and go as they wished. Many people, even those with very low support needs, became institutionalised and were given no opportunities to do anything, or choose anything for themselves.

Defining normalisation: the Scandinavian roots

The majority of the literature concerning normalisation acknowledges that the roots of the approach lie with the *Danish Mental Retardation Act* of 1959, which aimed to *'create an existence for the mentally retarded as close to normal living conditions as possible'* (Bank-Mikkelsen, 1980).

According to Bank-Mikkelsen, the objective of 'making normal' was extended to housing, education, work and leisure, all built on an underlying theme of campaigning for the equality of human and legal rights for *everyone*. Throughout the 1960s, thinking like this led to major developments in learning disability services in Denmark and Sweden. The aim became to:

'(make) *available to all mentally retarded people patterns of life and conditions of everyday living which are as close as possible to the regular circumstances and ways of life of society'*.

Nirje, 1980

In practice, this required that people with learning disabilities be enabled to experience the 'norms' of everyday life. For example, experiencing the rhythm of the day (we go to bed at night and get up in the mornings) and the rhythm of the week (most people work during the week and rest at the weekend).

Normalisation also demanded that we recognise that people with learning disabilities pass through the life cycle like others in the general population, have the right to form relationships and to experience an acceptable standard of living.

Developing the idea of normalisation: Wolfensberger's definition

The social and political environment in the USA was receptive to the ideas of normalisation, leading to widespread acceptance of the approach. Developments in civil rights activism, along with the acceptance by the Federal Courts of the '*least restrictive alternative*' approach to psychiatric care helped a sociologist named Wolf Wolfensberger to formulate his ideas. His central definition of normalisation is:

'*…the utilisation of means which are as culturally normative as possible, in order to establish and/or maintain personal behaviors and characteristics which are as culturally normative as possible*'.

Wolfensberger initiated two important changes to the approach.

1 He refers to the way in which **society** views and represents people with disabilities.

2 He emphasises 'socially valued roles' – this led to the later renaming of normalisation by Wolfensberger as **social role valorisation (SRV)**.

Wolfensberger's normalisation therefore became a way of encouraging services to create a positive image for and with people with learning disabilities, aimed at decreasing their stigmatisation and increasing their acceptance by wider society.

Normalisation in Britain

The climate became right for the acceptance of normalisation in Britain in a similar way to events leading up to its establishment in North America. In addition, a series of scandals provoking investigations into living conditions in a number of long-stay institutions enabled normalisation to influence the design of new service provision, as well as the modification of existing institutions.

During the 1970s and 1980s, organisations such as the Campaign for Mentally Handicapped People and King's Fund built on evidence from research to provide strong support for an approach that advocated 'ordinary' lives for people with learning disabilities. Interpretations of normalisation in Britain tend to use **John O'Brien's five service accomplishments** to inform services:

1 **Community presence:** ensuring that service users are present in the same parts of the community as people without disabilities, be it at work or in recreational activity

2 **Choice:** supporting people in making choices about their lives in as many areas and including as many issues as possible

3 **Competence:** encouraging the development of skills and abilities that are meaningful to the immediate culture, skills that decrease a person's dependency and are valued by non-disabled people

4 **Respect:** increasing the respect given to service users by other members of the community by ensuring that the lifestyles of people with learning disabilities encourage a positive image to be conveyed to others. This might refer to the clothes that people wear, the places they go to, and the way that support staff talk to service users

5 **Participation:** supporting people with learning disabilities in sustaining relationships with members of their family, as well as forming new relationships with others – ie making sure that '*service users* participate *in the life of the community.*'

O'Brien's work can be said to be different from that of Wolfensberger only in that he leaves out references to sociological theory, and concentrates on **quality of life** and **lifestyle**.

Age-appropriateness

Services for people with learning disabilities throughout Britain share a common goal: to support the integration of people with learning disabilities into the local community. Linked with this is the idea of age-appropriateness – treating adults with learning disabilities *as adults*. Historically, people with learning disabilities were denied certain rights as adults, such as the right to make choices, the right to live a sexual life and the right to respect. Age-appropriateness is a way of ensuring that the support offered to people is appropriate to the individual's *age*.

Examples of age-appropriate support

- When the individual achieves something, saying '*Well done* [person's name]!' (rather than saying '*Good boy/girl!*')

- Setting up systems within a residential service whereby people are supported to buy their own food and pay their own rent (rather than food arriving in bulk and bills being paid by staff without any involvement of service users)

- People wearing clothes worn by people of their age in the general population (rather than an individual in their fifties wearing jogging bottoms and trainers all the time because it is easier for staff to support the person getting dressed)

The pros and cons

Age-appropriateness has been valuable in helping people with learning disabilities to gain a more positive image in society and access opportunities that are available to people *without* disabilities. The closure of institutions has made people with learning disabilities more visible, making it even more important for the general public to be educated about this particular section of the community.

However, it is also important that people with learning *dis*abilities are respected for their *abilities*. There is a risk that by emphasising age-appropriateness above everything else, individuals with learning disabilities can be excluded from participating in activities and other aspects of community life because – for them – it is not meaningful.

The developmental approach

A way of tackling the thorny issue of age-appropriateness is to always have respect for the individual at the forefront of your mind. Respect for the individual means respecting *their* understanding of the world and the skills they have acquired for interacting with the environment. For example, people with severe and profound learning disabilities, because of the level of their disabilities, are at the very early stages of development. While they are adults and have lived a lifetime of experiences as an adult, the ways in which they understand the world and interact with it are at a level that can be compared with somebody much younger. Being aware of an individual's level of social and intellectual development is part of a person-centred approach to supporting them: starting with *who* the person is and *how* they can best be supported.

Summary   From birth, learning disability affects the way that people think and learn, and results in them needing varying levels of support to participate in daily life. The ways in which people with learning disabilities have been supported has changed dramatically throughout history. A major change has been the shift from segregated containment ('keeping' men and women separate from each other and society) and block treatment to the more recent individualised approach that aims to place the person with learning disabilities and his/her needs and skills at the centre of any support that is provided.

The challenge for those working in services for people with learning disabilities is to provide support that strikes a balance between treating the individual appropriately as an adult, and ensuring that s/he can access the environment in meaningful ways. How this can best be done will be explored in later chapters in this reader.

Further reading

Brown, H. & Smith, H. (Eds) (1992) *Normalisation: A reader for the nineties*. London: Routledge.

Emerson, E., Hatton, C., Felce, D. & Murphy, G. (2000) *Learning Disabilities: The Fundamental Facts*. London: Mental Health Foundation.

Myers, F., Ager, A., Kerr, P. & Myles, S. (1998) Outside looking in? Studies of the community integration of people with learning disabilities. *Disability & Society* **133** (3) 389–343.

Oliver, M. (1990) *The Politics of Disablement*. London: Macmillan.

References

Bank-Mikkelsen, N. (1980) Denmark. In: R. J. Flynn and K. E. Nitsch (Eds) *Normalisation, Social Integration and Community Services*. Austin, Texas: Pro-Ed.

Nirje, B. (1980) The Normalisation Principle. In: R. J. Flynn and K. E. Nitsch (Eds) *Normalisation, Social Integration and Community Services*. Austin, Texas: Pro-Ed.

This outdoor sculpture was part of a project run by ActionSpace for young learning disabled people in Camden. The people made a number of site-specific outdoor sculptures.

WRITTEN BY
Alison Brammer

Chapter 2

IN CONTEXT

KEY WORDS

collaborative working

Future Needs
Assessment

paternalistic

policy initiatives

Quality Protects

Policy and legislation

In order to be effective in working collaboratively with people with learning disabilities and their families, we need to be fully aware of the legal and policy context within which we are working. This chapter sets out the key legislative and policy initiatives that are likely to have direct impact upon the lives of people with learning disabilities, and summarises their main characteristics. It also contains a brief account of different service models for both children and adults with learning disabilities.

 Key point:

Developing a 'rights'-based approach

The law has tended to take a rather paternalistic stance towards people with learning disabilities, focusing on service provision. However, recent developments in the form of the *Disability Discrimination Act 1995* and the *Human Rights Act 1998* may promote and encourage development of a rights-based approach within law and practice affecting people with learning disabilities.

Legislation and service provision for children with learning disabilities

Legislation

1 Children Act 1989

The *Children Act 1989* was a major piece of reforming legislation. The central feature of the Act is **the welfare principle**, which states that the child's welfare is the court's most important consideration. It also places great emphasis on the provision of local authority support for children and their families, so as to enable children to remain living with their families and avoid the need for formal proceedings. Support is targeted at 'children in need', which includes children with disabilities. Local authorities are required to '*provide services designed… to minimise the effect on disabled children… of their disabilities, and to give such children the opportunity to lead lives as normal as possible*'.

These responsibilities are enhanced by the Quality Protects initiative (1998) which includes a range of objectives and performance indicators for local authorities.

Key point: Children Act 1989

Particularly relevant to children with disabilities is objective 6, which aims to ensure '...*children with specific social needs arising out of a disability are living in families or other appropriate settings in the community where their assessed needs are adequately met and reviewed'.*

2   Education Act 1993 (Part III) and 1996 (Part IV)

Education law is complex and rapidly changing.

Key point: Education Act 1993

A key provision is the requirement that local authorities and schools identify, assess, record, meet and review special educational needs.

Other agencies must contribute to this process. A revised Special Educational Needs Code of Practice is due to be implemented in early 2002 to take account of new SEN provisions of the *Special Educational Needs and Disability Act.* The Act and Code emphasise the importance of both working in partnership with parents, and pupil participation. In future, a statement will normally only be issued when provision cannot reasonably be provided within normal resources. It is presumed that a child with special educational needs should normally have their needs met in a mainstream setting.

Legislation in Northern Ireland is similar to that in England and Wales. The *Education Act (Northern Ireland Order) 1996* has similar characteristics to its counterpart. In **Scotland**, special educational needs are governed by the *Education (Scotland) Act 1981*. Children with more significant difficulties undergo Recording, a process similar to 'statementing'. Before leaving school, children have **a Future Needs Assessment** instead of a transition plan as used in England and Wales.

Provision for children with learning disabilities

Pre-school services

Children with learning disabilities are referred to child development units run by NHS trusts. Multidisciplinary assessments are offered with input from, for example, speech and language therapy, clinical psychology, educational psychology, occupational therapy and physiotherapy. Some areas have Portage schemes that employ specialist workers to implement structured programmes for children and their families.

Education services

Some educational authorities support children with learning disabilities in a range of special schools. Other authorities are increasingly advocating integration into mainstream schools including pupils with severe disabilities. The nature of integration in practice varies from school to school, and can include specialist units that offer opportunities for social integration through to full integration where the child with learning disabilities works to an individualised curriculum – drawn up specifically for them – within the mainstream classroom.

Family support

Support is given in the form of **short-term breaks** (formerly known as respite care). Children spend one or more nights away from the family in a staffed residential service or with another family in a linked scheme. Due to high demand, these services are often under considerable pressure to provide the support needed. Each local authority should maintain a register of disabled children that should influence the planning and provision of services in the area.

Legislation, policy and service provision for adults with learning disabilities

NHS and Community Care Act 1990

 Key point: NHS and Community Care Act 1990

This Act has six main objectives:

1   To promote a range of services that enable people to live in their own homes wherever possible and appropriate

2   To prioritise practical support for carers

3   To provide community care-based assessment of individual need

4   To work across agencies to provide a comprehensive service

5   To establish responsibility and accountability for provision

6   To ensure value for money

Local authorities are under a duty to carry out an assessment of anyone who appears to be in need of community care services, referred to as a **care/needs assessment**.

It is unlikely that the local authority will be able to refuse to carry out an assessment and it should be completed within a reasonable time. The individual's assessed needs will then be considered against the authority's eligibility criteria and a range of services may be offered, as part of a care plan. This might include, for example, social work support, home adaptations, meals on wheels, and occupational activities. The whole process of assessment, provision of services and review or reassessment is referred to as '**care management**'.

If the person is 'disabled' (ie blind, deaf or dumb, suffering from mental disorder of any description, handicapped by illness or injury), the local authority must also offer an assessment for services specified in the ***Chronically Sick and Disabled Persons Act 1970***. Guidance advises that services for adults with learning disabilities should be arranged on an individual basis, taking account of *'age, needs, degree of disability, the personal preferences of the individual and his or her parents or carers, culture, race and gender'*.

The local authority is entitled to make reasonable charges for services which they arrange or provide. As an alternative to direct provision of services, a local authority may make **direct payments** to an individual which enable the individual to purchase community care services themselves, provided that individual appears capable of managing a direct payment by themselves or with assistance.

Where care is provided to an individual on a regular but unpaid basis, the carer is also entitled to an assessment of their needs under the ***Carers (Recognition of Services) Act 1995***. Direct payments to carers (instead of providing services to assist the carer) are authorised under the ***Carers and Disabled Children Act 2000***.

Mental Health Act 1983

> **Key point:** *Mental Health Act 1983*
>
> This Act contains powers of compulsory admission and detention in hospital which may be exercised in limited circumstances when it is in the interest of the person concerned, or of wider society, and the mental health difficulties of the patient meet set criteria.

Many of the functions under the Act are given to a specially trained social worker known as an **Approved Social Worker**. The Act also authorises treatment of a mental disorder and prevents such action being considered false imprisonment and/or assault – even though treatment is without consent in certain circumstances. The Act is supported by a Code of Practice. New mental health legislation to replace the 1983 Act has been proposed and is expected in the near future. It contains proposals for a new **Community Treatment Order**.

Mental incapacity is frequently confused with mental illness and disorder. The issue of mental capacity is crucial in terms of personal autonomy and decision-making. For some people with learning disabilities, capacity to make certain decisions may be limited. This is a complex area and new laws recommended by the Law Commission are anticipated. Under current law it is important that all steps are taken to empower and enhance each individual's decision-making capacity.

The capacity required is the ability to reach an informed decision, by understanding information, weighing it in the balance and arriving at a decision.

For significant decisions, the High Court may make a declaration as to whether a proposed course of action is lawful. This process has been utilised to authorise the sterilisation of women with learning disabilities, as well as other medical treatment, and also to determine where a person shall live. If a person with a learning disability does not have the capacity to conduct legal proceedings, a 'litigation friend' may be appointed to act on their behalf.

Care Standards Act 2000

 Key point: *Care Standards Act 2000*

This provides for the regulation and inspection of residential accommodation and domiciliary services. This Act replaces the *Registered Homes Act 1984*.

A new National Care Standards Commission, independent of local or health authorities, will undertake the regulation function and national standards are being devised to ensure all services satisfy minimum levels.

The existence of abuse of adults, including adults with learning disabilities, is clearly established by research and has been recognised in practice and policy. Guidance – entitled *No Secrets* – exists, and requires local authorities to have procedures in place to identify and respond to adult abuse, commonly referred to as Adult Protection Guidelines. One strategy for preventing abuse is ensuring that unsuitable people do not work closely with vulnerable adults. The **Protection of Vulnerable Adults** list (POVA) is established under the *Care Standards Act* and held by the Department of Health. Care providers must refer a person to the list if there are concerns over conduct which has harmed or placed a vulnerable adult at risk of harm. Providers are also obliged to refer to the list before offering a position of employment.

Disability Discrimination Act 1995

 Key point: *Disability Discrimination Act 1995*

This prohibits discrimination against a person with a disability in employment, access and provision of goods and services.

A person is discriminated against if he is treated less favourably than a person who is not disabled.

Disability, for these purposes, **is defined as**:

'a physical or mental impairment which has a substantial and long term adverse effect on the ability to carry out normal day to day activities. A Disability Rights Commission supports the legislation and may conduct investigations'.

Human Rights Act 1998

 Key point: *Human Rights Act 1998*

The *Human Rights Act* came into force in 2000. It brings the rights and freedoms contained in the European Convention of Human Rights into domestic law.

The effect of the Act is that all laws must be interpreted by the courts, so as to comply with the Articles of the Convention. It is unlawful for a public authority (including local authorities and the police) to act in a way that is incompatible eg by denying a person's freedom of expression.

Previously, if a person suffered inhuman or degrading treatment or their right to family life was violated, it might have been necessary to complain to the European Court. The courts in the UK can now deal with such complaints. A number of areas of law have already been found in breach of the Convention, including aspects of the *Mental Health Act*. It is likely that further breaches will be identified and prompt law reform. The Act presents an important opportunity to establish a rights-based culture for all members of society.

Policy documents

Before *Valuing People* (Department of Health, 2001), the two main policy documents addressing the needs of people with learning disabilities were:

- *Health Services for Adults with Learning Disabilities* both
- *Social Care for Adults with Learning Disabilities* (both Department of Health, 1992).

Others include:

- the *Mansell Report* (1993) – which sets an agenda for provision supporting people with challenging behaviour and/or mental health needs
- publications stemming from *Our Healthier Nation*, which raised awareness of the need to support the health of vulnerable groups.

Valuing People (2001) is the first government strategy for learning disability produced by the Government since the 1971 white paper, *Better Services for the Mentally Handicapped*. **It has four key principles**:

- rights

- independence

- choice

- inclusion.

The white paper sets out an agenda for change with an overall objective of addressing the social exclusion of people with learning disabilities. The strategy does not envisage any specific areas of law reform.

Provision for adults with learning disabilities

Any provision should reflect individual choice as far as possible. The support of advocacy services and the principle of empowerment can promote this in reality.

Residential services

About half of all adults with learning disabilities live with their families, with the other half using residential provision. Community Care legislation is partly responsible for the expansion of residential services within the private and voluntary sectors. The current models of provision include the following:

Village communities

These are managed by the voluntary or private sectors. They tend to have provision for large numbers (50+ people), often in rural settings, but can be smaller and urban.

Hostels

These are medium-sized (10–25 places) and usually run by social services. They can be purpose-built or in converted large houses. Their number is falling. Research suggests the quality of support offered is better than in institutions but does not always conform to the principles of ordinary living.

Group homes/staffed housing

These are smaller, 'ordinary' houses (2–8 places), historically run by health and social services but increasingly run by the voluntary and private sector. Staffed houses can support people with high support needs. The support offered in group homes is generally of a higher quality than that available in larger settings, although there is considerable variance.

Supported living

This term is used to describe housing that is based upon the principles of separating accommodation from support. Typically, it involves people living alone as named tenants in ordinary flats and houses, but could involve sharing with others. More research is needed to assess the effectiveness of such arrangements.

Specialist residential services

These services aim to support particular characteristics or needs. Examples include: people with challenging behaviour, people at risk of offending, people with multiple disabilities and people with mental health problems. It is likely that this sector is expanding. Again, little evidence has emerged to enable assessment of effectiveness.

Day services

Historically, people with learning disabilities attended purpose-built day centres run by social services, arriving by special transport between normal working hours, Monday to Friday. The appropriateness of these centres has been questioned.

Increases in flexibility mean that adults with learning disabilities can access further education and employment opportunities available to the rest of the population, with individualised support. Accessibility and quality of such arrangements vary greatly according to where you live, while the complexities of the benefit system and their impact can affect the ways in which people with learning disabilities get paid for their efforts.

Family and individual support services

Short-break services are also available to adults with learning disabilities and their families, but again, demand tends to outstrip supply. Community-based support from multidisciplinary community teams can contribute to the design of individualised support, but availability and quality are likely to vary according to local issues and resources. For some people, home care or home help may be provided and outreach support can provide a variety of support.

Summary   All supporters of people with learning disabilities need to be familiar – and keep up to date – with the legislative framework within which they work, and the residential and other service options that are available. Ensure that you and your colleagues are informed, and find ways of passing key points on to the people you support. They have a right to know just how changes in law and policy will be affecting their daily lives.

© Pavilion, 2002   35

Further reading

Department of Health (1999) *No Secrets: The protection of vulnerable adults: Guidance on the development and implementation of multi-agency policies and procedures.* London: DoH.

Home Office (1998) *Speaking Up For Justice: Report of the Interdepartmental Working Group on the Treatment of Vulnerable or Intimidated Witnesses in the Criminal Justice System.* London: Home Office.

Cooper, J. (Ed) (2000) *Law, Rights and Disability.* London: Jessica Kingsley.

Clements, L. (1996) *Community Care and the Law.* London: Legal Action Group.

Key pieces of legislation

Chronically Sick and Disabled Persons Act 1970

Education (Scotland) Act 1981

Mental Health Act 1983

Children Act 1989

NHS and Community Care Act 1990

Education Act 1993 (Part III) and 1996 (Part IV)

Carers (Recognition of Services) Act 1995

Disability Discrimination Act 1995

Education Act (Northern Ireland Order) 1996

Human Rights Act 1998

Carers and Disabled Children Act 2000

Care Standards Act 2000

WRITTEN BY
Jennie Williams,
Frank Keating, and
Zenobia Nadirshaw

Chapter 3

ALL DIFFERENT, ALL EQUAL

KEY WORDS

anti-oppressive practice
discrimination
empowerment practice
equitable
gender-blind
gendered analysis
oppression
social isolation
practitioners
prevalence
punitive
social inequality

Understanding and developing anti-oppressive practice

Most people recognise that once a person is labelled as having a learning disability they are at risk of social exclusion, disadvantage and discrimination (Department of Health, 2001). What is considerably less well appreciated is the fact that these same people can *also* encounter oppression because of their gender, 'race', class and sexuality. Like everyone else, their lives are shaped by the existence of social inequalities in society. It is against this background that we are going to define anti-oppressive practice, explain why it is needed, and, finally, discuss the implications for action.

Defining anti-oppressive practice

Oppression can manifest itself in individual actions, organisational procedures and practices and how services are organised and delivered. Oppression therefore affects:

- how practitioners behave towards service users
- how people with learning disabilities come to services and the barriers to access these
- how services are organised and delivered to people with learning disabilities.

> Anti-oppressive practice comprises a set of beliefs, knowledge, and practices aimed at reducing the impact of inequality on the lives of service users and sensitivity is needed within service delivery (Di Terlizzi & Cambridge, 1999).

The starting place for anti-oppressive practice is a solid understanding of the many ways that social inequalities can affect both the lives and needs of people with learning disabilities, and also how services respond to these needs. Unfortunately, this solid understanding hasn't yet been established within services. This is partly because there is not a great deal of research literature that looks at the implications of social inequalities. It is also because establishing anti-oppressive practice in services can be both personally and professionally challenging, and good quality

training and supervision is not widely available. In the book, *Practising Equality*, Phillipson (1992) observes:

'anti-oppressive practice works with a model of empowerment and liberation and requires a fundamental rethinking of values, institutions and relationships'.

The basis of anti-oppressive practice

We shall focus here on the implications of disability, 'race' and gender. These examples will help alert us to the implications of other dimensions of oppression including those based on class, sexuality and age.

39

Learning disability and oppression

Most people working in services are well aware of the ways that social discrimination and disadvantage can shape the lives of people who are labelled as having a learning disability. Indeed, normalisation theory would not have become so influential without this recognition. People with learning disabilities have been identified as one of the most **vulnerable** and **socially excluded** group of individuals in our society. This is highlighted by some of the findings presented in the recent white paper on learning disability services (Department of Health, 2001), which pointed out the following...

Examples:

- Families with a child with a learning disability are likely to have higher costs (eg cases where the child needs support 24 hours a day) and parents may find it difficult to get work because of these added commitments.

- Young people with learning disabilities do not receive adequate support to make the transition to adult life.

- Most people with learning disabilities have little choice in and control over their lives.

- A substantial number of the health care needs of people with learning disabilities go unmet.

- The number of people with learning disabilities who live in independent housing is relatively small and social isolation remains a problem.

These findings alert us to some of the important ways in which people with learning disabilities are disadvantaged by, and excluded from society.

'Race' and ethnicity and oppression

There is no comprehensive research that can help us reliably gauge the incidence and prevalence of learning disabilities across the minority ethnic communities in Britain. There are, however, indications that the prevalence may be higher amongst some of these communities.

For example: the prevalence of learning disability in some South Asian communities has been found to be up to three times greater than in the general population.

It would be unwise to try and give meaning to such findings without taking into account the many ways in which people from black and minority ethnic communities experience discrimination in a wide range of areas in their lives.

Examples:

Black and minority ethnic communities…

- have higher rates of unemployment than white people (Commission for Racial Equality/CRE, 1997a)

- are over-represented in the criminal justice system (CRE, 1997b)

© Pavilion, 2002

- are more likely to be excluded from school

- have poorer access to well paid work, and poorer access to state benefits compared with white counterparts with similar needs (Nadirshaw, 2000).

Building a picture of the possible effects of racial and other inequalities on the life of a person is an essential first step in developing **empowerment practice**. But it is also very important to be aware of the many ways in which inequality can impact upon service provision itself. Evidence to date suggests that most services have been uninterested or unsuccessful in taking racial inequality into account, and that racism continues unchallenged within service provision and practice. Service users and carers from minority ethnic communities are often socially excluded by language barriers and racism, and subjected to negative stereotypes and attitudes.

1 **Carers from ethnic minority communities can be seriously disadvantaged because they lack crucial knowledge** about the range of learning disability services that are available, their rights to a community care assessment, and how to make a complaint.

2 **Diagnosis of learning disability is often made at a later age** than for the population as a whole and parents receive less information about their child's disability and the support available.

3 Carers frequently encounter services that **underestimate their attachments to cultural traditions** and religious beliefs.

4 Services are at risk of relying on **stereotypes** and **generalisations**, such as, 'they care for their own'.

5 **Socio-economic disadvantage and financial insecurity can also add significantly to carers' experience of stress**, isolation, and marginalisation.

6 People from minority ethnic communities with a learning disability are at a **higher risk of being diagnosed as having challenging behaviour**, due to stereotyped views and perceptions. They are therefore more likely to be offered more punitive treatments, such as exclusion.

Such limitations in service provision to ethnic minority communities are becoming more widely acknowledged. The government Learning Disability Strategy *Valuing People* (Department of Health, 2001) highlights the fact that the needs of black and minority ethnic people with learning disabilities are different, and have to be addressed through the provision of appropriate services.

Gender and oppression

Over the last 30 years there has been increased recognition that gender is a powerful part of our lives and experience. However, people with learning disabilities are often excluded from this debate (McCarthy, 1999). The implications of gender for **women** have attracted the greatest attention from researchers and practitioners. For example:

1 There is evidence from around the world that, compared to men, women have less access to resources such as money, status, value, power, leisure, social support and validation (Equal Opportunities Commission/EOC, 2000). We need to know what this means in terms of the lives of women using and working in services for people with learning disabilities; the absence of hard evidence shouldn't stop us asking obvious questions...

- Are women and men in our service receiving the same benefits or pay?

- Are women doing more than their fair share of domestic work?

- Is there gender bias in access to services, help, work, and leisure?

- Does the equal opportunity policy apply to service users as well as staff?

- Are there opportunities for women in this service to talk together about their lives?

- What equality issues are on the top of their agenda?

2   Inequality and injustice thrive when they are hidden. It is, therefore, reasonable to ask how inequality is hidden or disguised in services.

- Do we blame the victim – those who are most vulnerable and disadvantaged?

- Do we describe behaviour as 'challenging' (Burns, 2000; Di Terlizzi *et al*, 1999) or as 'mental illness' (Downie, 2001) when it would be more appropriate to consider it as a response to the impact or constraints of gender or race?

3   The existence of inequalities creates opportunities for very serious abuses of power. Again, there is global evidence that physical and sexual violence and abuse are commonplace, perpetrated overwhelmingly by men. There is a lot of well-developed work on gender within the field of learning disability which has recognised that this section of the population is particularly vulnerable.

4 Gender is the core component of our identity; it gives us a sense of ourselves as male or female. Yet most of the thinking that shapes services is gender-blind (see **Glossary**) so too are most of the conversations held about, and with, people with learning disabilities.

Learning disability is the main identity that structures services and interactions. This may make service provision easier, but does not help service users in their continuing struggle to assert or define themselves as women or men. However, taking gender into account when working with people with learning disabilities greatly increases the likelihood that we will meet their needs, and also understand how they cope with their difficulties.

Finally, there are already well-established attempts to strengthen the collective voice of women with learning disabilities (Atkinson *et al*, 2000). These include the work of the group Women in Learning Disability (Walmsley, 1997) and the Powerhouse Collective (Powerhouse, 1996).

Beyond labels People working within the field of learning disability should also borrow enthusiastically and critically from anti-oppressive practice and social action developed elsewhere. This will enable us to identify common threads in our lives and experiences, and to reduce the significance of difference defined by client group membership.

Implications for practice

There are a number of important implications for practice that can be drawn from the information presented here as well as the wider literature on empowerment practice. Empowerment practice is not possible unless we appreciate and try to understand the effects of oppression on the lives of people with learning disabilities and their carers. We must be familiar with key concepts such as power, powerlessness, privilege and disadvantage. The challenge for practitioners is that service users may be oppressed on several grounds at the same time (Williams, 2000). Even if a learning disability is the most obvious basis for oppression, it is important to consider whether oppression is taking place as well, on grounds of, for example, class, sexuality, age, or race.

However, it is not only learning and thinking about power issues that are important; workers themselves need to be empowered through supervision and the culture of their workplace to use this knowledge. Empowerment practice is also grounded in a well-informed appreciation of the ways that learning disability services themselves have been shaped by social inequalities. This knowledge is essential to providing and developing services that promote rights, independence, choice and inclusion (Department of Health, 2001).

Not only does empowerment practice need to be well informed about the impact of social inequalities on individuals and services, it also needs to be **reflective**. As 'empowerment practitioners' **we need to continually question our work, and the ways in which we try to use our own power in the interests of people with learning disabilities and their carers.**

Conclusion We have a collective and individual responsibility to eliminate the impact of social inequalities on the lives of people with learning disabilities, their families and carers. Responsibility for action lies with practitioners, service providers and commissioners, trainers and educators, and policy makers. This action needs to be taken in the knowledge and belief that good care is *not* about treating everyone the same. It is about treating people as unique individuals whose lives and experiences have been shaped by social inequalities.

Further reading

Baxter, C., Poona, K. & Wad, L. (1990) *Double Discrimination: Issues and services for people with learning difficulties from black and minority ethnic communities*. London: King's Fund.

McCarthy, M. (2000) *Sexuality and Women with Learning Disabilities*. London: Jessica Kingsley.

Nadirshaw, Z. (1999) Editorial in Special Issue: Race, Ethnicity and Learning Disability. *Tizard Learning Disability Review* **4** (4) 2–5.

Thompson, N. (1998) *Promoting Equality: Challenging discrimination and oppression in human services*. Basingstoke: Macmillan.

References

Atkinson, D., McCarthy, M. & Walmsley, J. (2000) *Good Times, Bad Times: Women with Learning Disabilities Tell Their Stories*. Kidderminster: BILD.

Burns, J. (2000) Gender identity and women with learning disabilities: the third sex. *Clinical Psychology Forum* **137** March 11–15.

Commission for Racial Equality (1997a) *CRE Factsheet: Employment and unemployment*. London: CRE.

Commission for Racial Equality (1997b) *CRE Factsheet: Criminal justice in England and Wales*. London: CRE.

Department of Health (2001) *Valuing People: A new strategy for learning disability for the 21st century*. London: The Stationery Office.

Di Terlizzi, M., Cambridge, P. *et al* (1999) Gender, ethnicity and challenging behaviour: a literature review and exploratory study. *Tizard Learning Disability Review* **4** (4) 33–44.

Downie, S. (2001) Falling through the gap. *Feminist Review* **68** 177–180.

Equal Opportunities Commission (2000) *Women and Men in Britain at the Millennium*. Manchester: EOC.

McCarthy, M. (1999) Guest Editorial of Special Issue: Gender Matters. *Learning Disability Bulletin* **112** (March) 1–4.

Nadirshaw, Z. (2000) Learning disabilities in multi-cultural Britain. In: D. Bhugra and R. Cochrane (Eds) *Multi-cultural Psychiatry in Britain*. London: Gaskell Publications.

Phillipson, J. (1992) *Practising Equality: Women, men and social work*. London: CCETSW.

Powerhouse (1996) Power in the House: Women with learning difficulties organising against abuse. *Encounters with Strangers: Feminism and Disability*. J. Morris. London: Women's Press.

Walmsley, J. (1997) Including people with learning difficulties: theory and practice. (Chapter 4). In: L. Barton and M. Oliver. (Eds) *Disability Studies: Past, present and future*. Leeds: Disability Press.

Williams, J. (2000) Endnote from a social inequalities perspectiv. In: S. Baum and J. Burns (Eds) Meeting the needs of women with learning disabilities: the significance of gender. *Clinical Psychology Forum (Special Issue)* **137** 36–37.

WRITTEN BY
Paul Cambridge

Chapter 4

 # IN SAFE HANDS

KEY WORDS

generic

intermediary

infantilisation

depersonalisation

victimisation

dispossession

responsibility

neglect

*Protecting people
from abuse*

What we know

In the 1960s, critical studies (eg Townsend, 1962: Morris, 1969: Robb, 1967) fuelled widespread disquiet about the role of institutions, including the old mental handicap hospitals, and their associations with abuse. Martin (1984) defined **institutionalised abuse** as:

- individual callousness and brutality
- low standards and morale
- weak and ineffective leadership
- pilfering by staff
- vindictiveness towards complainants
- the failure of management to concern itself with abuse.

Such observations confirmed the connection between institutionalised care and controlling and punishing regimes made by others (Goffman, 1961), characterised by humiliation, dispossession and exclusion (Foucault, 1977).

Language and abuse

Abusive behaviour has also been attributed to attitudes towards people with learning disabilities (Wolfensberger, 1975). Sub-human language and images result in people being treated as children (**infantilisation**), in our not seeing people as individual or even human (**depersonalisation**) and exercising

power over them, in small, indeliberate ways, and in more obviously abusive ways (**victimisation**). This is reflected in the tendency to decriminalise offences committed against people with learning disabilities (Sobsey, 1994) in both the language used and the incapacity of the criminal justice system to meet their needs. **For example:** by using terms such as 'sexual abuse' which doesn't sound as shocking or real as terms like 'rape'; 'restraint' instead of 'assault', 'seclusion' instead of 'imprisonment' or 'sedation' instead of 'poisoning'.

Using language in this way can provide 'cover' for those wishing to abuse people with learning disabilities, distracting others from the seriousness of the acts committed.

Abuse and power

Others (Hollins, 1994) have explained abuse by looking at the nature of **dependency relationships**, with the risk of abuse increased by the gaps between user and carer needs, or particular models such as carer stress or social learning (Sobsey, 1994). Relative power and powerlessness have therefore repeatedly emerged as central features in abuse, both in relation to the perpetrators and victims, although so too have financial greed, cruelty and sadism.

Research

More is known about the incidence and prevalence of sexual abuse than any other form of abuse perpetrated against people with learning disabilities. Research on sexual abuse suggests that self-disclosure – people telling others that they have been abused – is the main source for alerting carers to abuse. Individual case studies suggest it is critical for facilitating the wider disclosure of abusive regimes. In recognition of this, there have been attempts to familiarise people with learning disabilities with court procedures (Hollins, 1994).

**Defining
vulnerability
and the
different types
of abuse**

 Adult vulnerability has been defined by the Law Commission, which states that a vulnerable adult is any person over the age of 18 who:

'is in need of community care services by reason of mental or other disability, age or illness and who is or may be unable to take care of himself or herself, or unable to protect himself or herself against significant harm or serious exploitation'.

Law Commission, 1995

 Adult abuse is defined as:

'physical, sexual, financial, emotional or psychological violation or neglect of a person unable to protect themselves or to prevent from happening or to remove themselves from abuse or potential abuse by others'.

Law Commission, 1995

Many agency policies on adult protection define the different categories of abuse and give examples of the signs and signals associated with each type.

> **Physical abuse**, for example, has been defined as:
>
> *'including injuries which are not explained satisfactorily, where there is concern that the injury was inflicted intentionally or through lack of care... Pushing, pinching, slapping, punching, and forced feeding would come into this category depending on the circumstances within which they occurred'.*
>
> Greenwich Social Services, 1993

In reality, however, different types of abuse can also happen in individual cases. **Emotional abuse**, in the form of threats and intimidation, is commonly associated with sexual abuse. **Financial abuse** may accompany sexual or physical abuse. A cross-section of London borough social services' adult-protection policies includes a range of categories of abuse:

- physical abuse
- physical neglect
- negligence in the face of unacceptable risk-taking behaviour
- sexual abuse
- financial abuse
- emotional abuse or neglect
- unauthorised administration of, or withdrawal of, prescribed medication
- unauthorised use of control and restraint, punishment or seclusion
- racial abuse
- psychological or social abuse.

Physical and sexual abuse are invariably prominent, reflecting both their severity and prevalence.

Most services for people with learning disabilities now have policies and guidelines on sexual abuse, recognising the vulnerability of people with learning disabilities to sexual abuse and exploitation (eg Greenwich Social Services, 1993). More recently, generic abuse, adult protection or vulnerable adults policies have been developed (eg Southwark Social Services, 1998).

Adult protection has been at the leading edge of social care policy development. It has been underpinned by a body of research and practice innovation in sexual abuse and learning disability, fuelled by abuse scandals in services for people with learning disabilities in the community (Cambridge, 1999). Increasingly, adult protection mirrors perspectives from child protection. This culminated in policy recognition at national level with *No Secrets* (Department of Health, 2000). *No Secrets* provides guidance on developing and implementing multi-agency policies and procedures to protect vulnerable adults from abuse, including:

- setting the scene and risk management (**what we know** using evidence from research)

- suggestions for setting up interagency frameworks ('**teamworking**', multi-agency working, roles and responsibilities, agency and officer lead and operation)

- developing **policies** and wider strategies (principles, training, commissioning, confidentiality)

- procedures for **responding** (investigations, record-keeping, disciplinary procedures, advocacy)

- **getting the message across** (recruitment, guidelines, volunteers, information).

Local authority social services departments have generally led adult protection policy and practice, due to their planning, co-ordinating and market-management role in community care, but the involvement of the police, with specialist vulnerable victims officers/co-ordinators, is important.

Protecting witnesses within the legal system

Speaking Up for Justice (Home Office, 1998) reported on the treatment of vulnerable witnesses in the criminal justice system giving evidence in court. Recommendations were incorporated into the *Youth Justice and Criminal Evidence Act 1999* and an implementation programme *Action for Justice* (Home Office, 2000). These two documents put in place measures designed to help intimidated witnesses. These changes will make it easier for people with learning disabilities to give evidence as competent witnesses, with special measures designed to help vulnerable witnesses give evidence. They are designed to reduce the experience of intimidation – feelings of being under pressure. The measures include:

- the assistance of an intermediary ('go-between')
- signing
- the permission to use unsworn evidence
- use of screens and video links
- video recordings of evidence
- clearing the court
- the removal of wigs and gowns.

Misuse of guidelines

Neglect, or **the breaking of care guidelines**, as categories of abuse in their own right, illustrate a **potential relationship between abusive practice and poor quality care. For example:** inappropriate physical interventions in response to violent challenging behaviours (Harris, 1996).

The misuse of control and restraint procedures has received considerable attention in relation to adult protection because they can harm the person (Spreat *et al*, 1986; Williams, 1995). These procedures have also received prominence in recent investigations.

See **Box 1** opposite.

> ### Box 1: Case study
>
> An influential Inquiry into the abuse of people with learning disabilities (Longcare, 1998) centred on independent provisions where residents had been systematically abused by the owner, including having their care and support withdrawn.
>
> Social services had continued to purchase from Longcare despite allegations of abuse, with the inspection and registration service failing to act on the conditions prevailing in the service.
>
> The recent television exposé of the abuse of people with learning disabilities and challenging behaviours in private care in Medway (MacIntyre, 1999) pointed to similar systems failures, although this was smaller scale.

Other areas of risk in adult protection lie closer to day-to-day practices. Intimate and personal care is an area of work which has also been associated with high risk situations, particularly in relation to the tension between privacy and accountability, duty of care and client consultation and the shortcomings of same-gender care policies. Whilst the latter may protect women with learning disabilities from sexual abuse, they leave men with learning disabilities open to this risk and do not address the risks of neglect and physical abuse.

Intimate care also confronts the sexuality of staff and service users through the exposure and touch of intimate and sexual body parts, raising questions about consent to touch.

What to look for

Organisations and settings

A number of factors are common to abusive cultures in services for people with learning disabilities in the community, and some are similar to those found in the past in hospitals, in particular:

- closed and inward-looking services and staff attitudes
- isolated and secretive organisations and services
- distant management style
- poor supervision, and
- intimidation and threats

have all been linked to abusive regimes (Longcare, 1998; Cambridge, 1999; MacIntyre, 1999).

Similar methodologies have been employed for defining the characteristics of potential victims and perpetrators in services for people with learning disabilities (see **Box 2**, below).

Box 2:

Characteristics of victims and perpetrators
(based on Sobsey 1994)

Characteristics of victims

- impaired defences
- impaired communication
- compliance
- low self-image

Characteristics of perpetrators

- the need for control
- displaced aggression
- low self-esteem
- little attachment to victims

Signs and signals

Using physical abuse as an example, there are particular signs and signals to watch for in people with learning disabilities. These include:

- unexplained injuries or bruises
- increases in the frequency, severity or duration of challenging behaviours
- withdrawal or mood swings
- fear of certain people or places.

Is it abuse?

A useful way to help us think about and define abuse is to consider whether actions or behaviours are *intended* to be abusive, at the same time as considering whether actions or behaviours are *experienced* as abusive. **Table 1** (below) summarises a formulation for defining suspected abuse. Unlike some approaches, it acknowledges that there are sometimes no clear lines between abuse and consent, and we do not always have the information available to help us act decisively.

Table 1 Deconstructing the boundaries between abuse and consent			
Categories of intent and experience	**Intended as abusive**	**Not intended as abusive**	**Impossible to ascertain intent**
Experienced as abusive	Clearly abuse	Probably abuse	Should be initially treated as abuse
Not experienced as abusive	Probably abuse	Clearly not abuse	Probably not abuse
Impossible to ascertain how experienced	Should be initially treated as abuse	Probably not abuse	Impossible to tell whether or not abuse

Adapted and developed from McCarthy & Thompson (1994)

Responsibility   Services need to fine-tune the support for clients and staff in responding to abuse, neglect and mistreatment. Often, responsibility has stopped with frontline staff, when there are wider issues of competence that need to be addressed. For example, developing individualised approaches to communication with service users; making high risk situations or challenging areas of practice visible in recruitment and supervision; and developing individual guidelines which tell staff how to support individuals well, rather than simply listing tasks (Cambridge & Carnaby, 2000).

What to do   Most policies and procedures will have clear information on how to report any concerns about abuse and what to do and not to do in particular instances, including action to protect the potential victim and not to alert the potential perpetrator (see *AIMS for Adult Protection* packs, Brown, 1998).

The different stages in the adult protection process will usually include:

- completing an alert
- reporting your concerns
- a planning meeting for an investigation
- undertaking an investigation
- sharing the findings at a case conference
- monitoring and evaluating progress.

Who is involved in each stage will be determined by the adult protection team, investigator or manager and sometimes the police will take responsibility for the investigation if there is a criminal aspect to the case. Of course, not all cases will follow the complete process and the process itself may not move through the steps described, as there may be feedback between the different stages – particularly if the case is complex.

Adult protection responsibilities will usually rest with a senior manager or community teams or named individuals, such as reporting officers or adult protection co-ordinators. Such procedures are required in order to help ensure that the evidence is effectively managed. Different types of evidence may have different significance and importance and include:

- forensic and medical evidence

- witness disclosures and statements via interviews

- circumstantial evidence

- self-disclosure and interviews with victim

- documentation and records.

How these different types of evidence generally emerge and fit into the investigation process will vary from case to case, hence the need for careful management and co-ordination. One particularly important consideration to emerge from various inquiries has been support for staff witnesses who disclose abuse, and such measures should be addressed in **whistle-blowing policies**.

Conclusions   Services and researchers have come together to look at how adult protection can be taken forward in commissioning services, and through functions such as inspection and registration.

Consideration has also been given to issues for implementing adult protection policies in local authorities.

With training materials such as the AIMS packs (1998), and codes of practice in important areas such as physical interventions, adult protection competence in services for people with learning disabilities is continuing to improve, built on early work in sexual abuse.

However, we need to continually improve preventative and early detection work and make sure the threshold to reporting abuse and the tolerance of abuse is low. This is sometimes difficult when staff and managers do not often have time for routine responsibilities, let alone taking on additional tasks.

Guidelines for supporting witnesses who blow the whistle on abuse need to be built into adult protection procedures and adopted by commissioning agencies. Staff and managers on adult protection training universally report a failure to effectively support whistleblowers, an observation also stemming from inquiries (Cambridge, 1999).

Such policies can:

- minimise the potentially negative emotional and psychological effects on the whistle-blower
- reduce the stress and anxiety related to involvement in subsequent investigations or legal action
- protect the person from negative economic or employment consequences
- give other potential witnesses the encouragement to disclose abuse.

Openness and accountability, with constructuve scrutiny and review of practice also help make services safer. Good recruitment, support and supervision systems for managers and staff, aligned with best practice, are among the most important preventative elements.

Most important of all, however, service users need access to effective individual planning, advocacy and education on sexuality, rights and assertiveness and, for those without a voice, individualised approaches to communication.

Having knowledge, a voice and the confidence to disclose abuse, whether to yourself or others, is real empowerment.

> ### Further reading
>
> Brown, H. (1998) *AIMs for Adult Protection: The Alerter's Training Pack*. Brighton: Pavilion.
>
> Brown, H., Stein, J. & Turk, V. (1995) The sexual abuse of adults with learning disabilities: report of a second two- year incidence survey. *Mental Handicap Research* **8** (1) 1–22.
>
> Cambridge, P. (1999) The first hit: a case study of the physical abuse of people with learning disabilities and challenging behaviours in a residential service. *Disability and Society* **14** (3) 285–308.
>
> Sobsey, D. (1994) *Violence and Abuse in the Lives of People with Learning Disabilities*. London: Brookes.

References

BILD (2001) *BILD Code of Practice for Trainers in the Use of Physical Interventions*. Kidderminster: BILD.

Brown, H. (1996) *Towards Safer Commissioning: A handbook for purchasers and commissioners*. Nottingham: NAPSAC.

Brown, H. (1999) *AIMs for Adult Protection: The Investigator's Training Pack*. Brighton: Pavilion.

Brown, H., Brammer, A., Craft, A. & McKay, C. (1996) *Towards Better Safeguards: A handbook for inspectors and registration officers*. Nottingham: NAPSAC.

Brown, H. & Stein, J. (1998) Implementing adult protection policies in Kent and East Sussex. *Journal of Social Policy* **27** (3) 371–396.

Foucault, M. (1977) *Discipline and Punish*. London: Allen Lane.

Goffman, E. (1961) *Asylums*. New York: Anchor.

Greenwich Social Services (1993) *Recognising and Responding to the Sexual Abuse of Adults with Learning Disabilities*. London: Greenwich Social Services and Greenwich Health Authority.

Harris, J. (1996) Physical restraint procedures for managing challenging behaviours presented by mentally retarded adults and children. *Research in Developmental Disabilities* **17** 99–134.

Hollins, S. (1994) Relationships between perpetrators and victims of physical and sexual abuse. In: J. Harris and A. Craft (Eds) *People with Learning Disabilities at Risk of Physical or Sexual Abuse*. Seminar Papers No. 4, Kidderminster: BILD.

Home Office (2000) *Action for Justice*. London: Home Office.

Law Commission (1995) *Report 231, Mental Incapacity*. London: HMSO.

Longcare (1998) *Independent Longcare Inquiry*. Buckinghamshire: County Council.

Martin, J. (1984) *Hospitals in Trouble*. Blackwell: Oxford.

McCarthy, M. & Thompson, D. (1994) *Sex and Staff Training*. Brighton: Pavilion.

Morris, P. (1969) *Put Away*. London: Routledge.

Robb, B. (1967) *Sans Everything: A case to answer*. London: Nelson.

Sanders, A., Creaton, J., Bird, S. & Weber, L. (1997) *Victims with Learning Disabilities: Negotiating the Criminal Justice System*. Occasional paper no. 17, Centre for Criminological Research, University of Oxford.

Spreat, S., Lipinski, D., Hill, J. & Halpin, M. (1986) Safety indices associated with the use of contingent restraint procedures. *Applied Research in Mental Retardation* **7** 475–481.

Southwark Social Services Department (1998) *Vulnerable Adults Policy*. London: Southwark Council.

Townsend, P. (1962) *The Last Refuge*. London: Routledge.

Wardhaugh, J. & Wilding, P. (1993) Towards an explanation of the corruption of care. *Critical Social Policy* **37** 4–31.

Williams, C. (1995) *Invisible Victims: Crime and abuse against people with learning difficulties*. London: Jessica Kingsley.

Wolfensberger, W. (1975) *The Origin and Nature of our Institutional Models*. Syracuse: Human Policy Press.

WRITTEN BY
Paul Cambridge

Chapter 5

TAKING THE RISK

KEY WORDS

informed risk-taking

risk assessment

risk management

exploitation

policies and policy
guidelines

*Assessing and
managing risk*

Risk **management** in services for people with learning disabilities happens along a continuum from 'informal' risk management to 'formal' risk management. Some things we do automatically, like stopping someone we know has no understanding of danger from crossing a busy main road on their own (**informal**). Other things we do in a considered way, such as supporting someone to boil a kettle and make a cup of tea, because, through assessment, we know they lack the appropriate skills (**formal**). Occasionally, risk-taking is referenced formally in policies, such as how to respond to minimising the risks of sexual activity, such as sexual abuse and HIV.

Why take risks? At one time, segregation in institutions was seen as the main way of managing the safety and security of people with learning disabilities (Alaszweski *et al*, 1999). However, risk management and risk-taking in community services for people with learning disabilities now mean helping service users develop their potential as individuals and become more independent. They are also central to some particular areas of practice – such as supporting people with challenging behaviours – and include assessing the risks to the person, other service users and staff. People with learning disabilities often lack the knowledge and experience to take **informed risks** – they may not be aware of exactly *what* the risk is, or *how* risky it is, cannot grasp the consequences of an activity. Services therefore have responsibilities beyond simply providing information or advice to clients.

Keeping records

Risk assessment is designed to identify the level and nature of risk. **Risk management** looks at the more complex relationships between risk-taking and other demands on services, such as the duty of care, responsibilities for protecting vulnerable people, and individual rights. It therefore usually leads to an action plan or intervention, with agreed responsibilities between people.

Such decisions should be part of the service user's individual plan and, sometimes, subject to the approval of managers or the guidance provided in policies. It is important to **record** all risk-taking decisions with the reasons for and against the course of action taken. The service will then be protected from claims of negligence if it can demonstrate that decisions involving risk were professionally and responsibly made. This is also basic to best practice.

In this chapter, HIV is used as a worked example to consider the issues inherent in risk management, the processes involved and the different approaches staff and services can take.

Basic risk management

Risk-taking is directly related to participation in life and taking up opportunities to develop as individuals, whatever an individual's level of learning disability. It would therefore be unrealistic to try to achieve a risk-free life for service users. Some lifestyle risks, such as those associated with smoking or diet, are increasingly being recognised as important for supporting people. Much will depend on what is made visible and said about risk-taking in regular policies and guidelines, individual plans and, occasionally, specific risk-taking policies.

Risk management has its roots in cost-benefit analysis, and has been more prominent in health than social care (Eby, 2000).

A basic model for risk management and decision-making in social care will usually include the following criteria or actions (developed from Carson, 1990).

■ Draw up lists of competing considerations ('pros' and 'cons') regarding the risk (benefits and costs) to the client.

■ Do the same for the staff or service (advantages and disadvantages).

■ Consider both the length of these lists as well as the relative importance and weighing up of the different factors.

■ Identify who is responsible for deciding and what model of decision-making is best (single worker, team, senior manager, director, specialist advisor).

- Consider the frequency of likely occurrence of the risk events.

- Identify any action that could be taken to reduce uncertainty.

- Consider the steps that could be taken to make the benefits or advantages more likely to occur.

- Consider long-term gains and risks against short-term gains and risks.

- Record the decisions made and responsibilities for the actions recommended.

Although the Jay Committee (Jay, 1979) and Social Services Inspectorate (Fruin, 1998) both stressed the importance of risk-taking and related policies, a study by Alaszewski and his colleagues (1999) also observed that only a small minority of agencies surveyed had risk or whistle-blowing policies. Key findings from this study also highlighted the different perceptions of risk on the part of service users, relatives and professionals, with the conclusion that effective risk policies should comprise:

- a clear statement of aims and the purpose of the policy

- a clear definition of risk, identifying issues, consequences and probability

- a clear statement of components, including planning and assessment, and decision-making

- recording a clear statement of policy and practice for risk management.

See **Case example** opposite.

Case example

Critical areas of practice for risk management

There are critical areas of practice where risk procedures have been, or may need to be, developed. For example, Harris and colleagues (1996) have developed procedures for the use of physical interventions. These provide a framework for risk management in other critical areas of practice, for example:

- challenging behaviour and physical interventions
- sexual abuse and capacity to consent
- sexual health and HIV
- intimate and personal care
- offending behaviours and dangerousness
- medical treatment and drug compliance
- substance misuse and drug use
- self harm and suicide
- cross dressing and gender identity
- cultural identity, race and appropriate support

HIV risk assessment   Without knowing the nature or level of risk, the risk cannot be effectively managed. In relation to HIV, we know the main ways HIV can be transmitted, providing the basic information we need to undertake HIV risk assessment.

Most HIV infections are transmitted through infected blood, semen or vaginal fluid. Therefore, the main potential and actual routes of infection are through:

- high HIV-risk sex (unprotected anal or vaginal sex, either as the insertive or receptive partner) with a person infected with HIV

- sharing needles for intravenous drug use (rather than using new, clean needles each time drugs are injected)

- medical procedures using contaminated blood, blood products or tissue (screening or treatment has now eliminated this in the developed world)

- vertical transmission from mother to child during pregnancy or childbirth.

In reality, we will need to know much more to undertake an effective HIV risk assessment in a particular risk area, such as sexuality. For example, detailed consideration would include recognising that:

- using a condom for penetrative vaginal or anal sex reduces but does not eliminate the risk of HIV infection. Condoms can split or come off during penetrative sex and the use of water-based lubricants and extra strong condoms for anal sex can help prevent this from happening

- the receptive partner is more at risk than the insertive partner

- anal sex is higher risk than vaginal sex

- oral sex is generally considered as very much safer than unprotected penetrative sex, even without the use of condoms, unless semen is exchanged or blood is present.

In Britain, most known cases of Aids and HIV infections are accounted for by men who have had sex with men. At the end of 1998, for example, men accounted for over 80% of the 33,000 known HIV infections. Transmission by sex between men accounted for 60% of infections, sex between men and women 20%, IV drug use 10% and contaminated blood/tissue 5% (NHPIS, 1999).

We also know other behavioural factors associated with HIV risk. Men who have sex with men remain the highest HIV risk group, although heterosexual transmissions now account for the majority of newly reported infections. Clearly, we would need to know a lot about someone's sexual life and encounters in order to undertake an effective HIV risk assessment, as key factors would include:

- type of sex (high risk if anal or vaginal penetrative sex, low risk if oral sex)

- whether condoms are used regularly and effectively (safer penetrative sex)

- frequency of unsafe sexual behaviours (the more frequent, the more risk of HIV)

- the risk group of the sexual partner (potentially higher if with men who have sex with men, people from Africa or IV drug users who share needles, for example)

- sex and safer sex education (knowledge of sex and safer sex)

- ability to practise safer sex (including assertiveness and negotiating skills)

- reported realities of sexual encounters (from keyworking or sex education).

In addition, **indirect indicators of risk** might need to be used to help assess the likelihood that sex and high HIV-risk sex might be taking place. For example, for men with learning disabilities who have sex with men without learning disabilities, various things might indicate that someone may be at increased risk, such as:

- being seen hanging around public toilets, parks or other places men meet to have sex

- talking about homosexuality or gay sex

- having a gay identity

- talking about friendships with other men

- being absent from the service for long periods without explanation

- having unexplained money or presents

- having an unexplained sexually transmitted infection

- being secretive or refusing to talk about activities.

The majority of men with learning disabilities at risk of HIV are also likely to be having sex with other men and women with learning disabilities, raising additional considerations for HIV risk assessment and management.

HIV risk management HIV infection is potentially a much less likely risk than sexual abuse (the prevalence of sexual abuse is known to be high). However, it is a potentially more serious risk, because life is invariably at stake and there are major social and economic costs, such as quality of life and drug treatments. HIV is also an easy risk to ignore, as high HIV-risk behaviours may be invisible (such as unsafe sex outside services), the consequences may be longer-term (long timescales between HIV infection and illness) and there are difficulties in attributing specific events to infection. Individual rights to sexual activity and opportunities for sexual expression have to be judged in relation to the risks involved for the person and others. Such considerations make HIV risk management decisions difficult.

Drawing a bold line between acceptable and unacceptable HIV risk is impossible, as people attach different values and benefits to risk-taking. However, services can ask some basic questions about people's understanding and appreciation of sex, safer sex and HIV. This helps to assess informed risk-taking and the nature of possible HIV preventive (risk management) activities.

- **Is the contact mutual or exploitative?** If it is exploitative, then there is a clear case for intervening to stop it, regardless of HIV risk.

- **Is the behaviour high risk?** If they are having unprotected anal or vaginal sex then there is clearly a significant risk to be managed, whereas oral sex or other sexual contact could be assessed as low risk and requiring a lower priority intervention.

- **Is the behaviour frequent or likely to reoccur?** A one-off medium to high-risk event is likely to require a very different response from a situation of repeated risk-taking, which is likely to continue.

- **Does the person at risk know about safer sex and are they physically able to practise it?** If not, then they should receive intensive safer sex education, have access to condoms and receive ongoing staff support and monitoring.

- **Is the person at risk able to insist on safer sex and that they or their partner(s) use condoms for high HIV risk activities such as penetrative anal or vaginal sex?** If not, then they should receive HIV counselling, intensive safer-sex education and training for assertiveness and negotiating skills.

Most responses will involve safer sex education and assertiveness work, but in some cases risk will be so high or knowledge so low, that short or long-term measures might need to be taken to restrict or eliminate high HIV risk behaviours. However, such decisions need to take account of rights and responsibilities at both the individual client and service levels. **Table 1** (overleaf) illustrates an increasingly complex level of decision-taking and risk-management in relation to HIV, for an individual case. Similarly, the potential legal risks for services will increase as the level of risk increases (Gunn, 1997).

Conclusions In summary, a number of possible HIV risk management responses can be identified:

- testing for HIV (see below)

- keeping someone at home

- escorting someone when out

- limiting someone's activities when at home

- providing safer sex education

- counselling for HIV

- referral to specialist GUM service

- referral to gay men's support/advocacy group.

The potential responses vary in their approach and acceptability and have various advantages and disadvantages, which will need to be considered on an individual basis. Simply encouraging a gay identity will not, for example, be a preferred option for many men with learning disabilities, who have sex with men who usually retain a heterosexual identity. The evidence from sex education suggests a wide gap between the knowledge and practice of safer sex for people with learning disabilities (McCarthy & Thompson, 1997). Restricting someone's activities might infringe their liberty or lead to an increase in challenging behaviour.

Table 1	Decision-making for HIV Risk Assessment and Risk Management	
Level of decision	**Examples of level of risk**	**Examples of decision-taking**
1	Change in known sexual behaviour raises possible sexual health issues Need for safer-sex education discussed as part of IPP*	Keyworker or support worker informs house manager and care manager
2	Referral for client to have safer-sex education HIV risk assessment undertaken Decision not to involve parents in discussion of client's sexuality at request of client	House manager in consultation with service manager with advice from sexuality co-ordinator
3	High HIV risk disclosed/assessed (client sometimes has unprotected insertive or receptive anal sex with men without learning disabilities) Assertiveness programme designed to help client negotiate and practice safer sex (basic HIV risk management) Safer-sex education continued and messages re-inforced and targeted at known high HIV risk behaviours and counselling re HIV risk and consequences	Service manager informs operations manager with advice from sexuality co-ordinator
4	Further disclosures through sex education that client sometimes has sex with other men and women with learning disabilities Decision to provide others with individual sex and safer sex education Local HIV risk management strategy developed	Meeting between house, service and operations manager and sexuality co-ordinator
5	Client requests HIV test and referred to specialist counselling GUM (Genito-Urinary Medicine, ie sexual health) clinic HIV risk management programmes for individual clients at risk established	Operations manager with advice from sexuality co-ordinator and ethical committee or independent advisor

*Individual Person Planning

HIV testing is potentially a very important part of HIV risk assessment and risk management. If an HIV test is thought necessary, then it may only legally be done if the individual can give **informed consent** to it. Without informed consent, an HIV test amounts to assault. To give informed consent (as opposed to saying yes) a person must not be encouraged or otherwise pressured to have the test and must appreciate the potential consequences and limitations. In particular they should:

- understand the nature of HIV/Aids

- appreciate the nature and limits of the HIV test

- be able to demonstrate why they want a test

- be able to consider confidentiality and disclosure

- appreciate the emotional and social consequences of testing positive or negative.

Testing for HIV

Only people with mild learning disabilities are likely to be able to give informed consent. If a test is considered without the individual's informed consent, this must be legally sanctioned by a court of law. Moreover, counselling would need to be provided and protocols for managing confidentiality would need to be in place.

Policies and practice

At a more general level, risk management policies and procedures can help, but these need to be accessible and practical for service managers and staff to use effectively. One way of doing this is for risk management to be fully placed within specific policies that relate to the area of practice. For example, risks that relate to HIV can be addressed through sexuality policies (Cambridge & McCarthy, 1997) or specific HIV policies (Horizon, 1996).

Summary Guidelines for risk management in services for people with
learning disabilities need to empower staff and managers to take
positive risks in relation to supporting service users in routine
things (such as developing life skills) and more complex things
(such as increasing their independence and participating in the
community).

*The following checklist should help achieve a working relationship
between promoting individual rights and protecting people from
danger – and enable services to develop a positive culture of
risk-taking.*

For every risk situation it is important to think about the
following points:

- the potential benefits or gains to the person's functioning,
  quality of life and life experience *as well as* the risks to the
  person and the service

- the costs to services and staff *as well as* to service users of
  perpetuating institutionalised dependency relationships
  through a reluctance to take risks

- the learning and mutual respect that can be developed
  between staff and service users from supporting positive
  risk-taking in people's lives

- the risks of developing a culture of introspection (ie self-
  scrutiny) through excessively defensive management and
  practice.

Every risk, whether routine and low level (such as boiling a
kettle), or higher level (such as road safety and HIV), can be
addressed through a basic risk assessment in a person's individual
plan, with actions and responsibilities made clear. However, not
all risk-taking will necessarily have positive outcomes, otherwise

it would not be risk-taking. The objective is to minimise risk and maximise gain. In so doing we also need to consider the support that both staff and service users may need if risk-taking goes wrong. Learning from negative as well as positive outcomes of risk-taking can happen at case review and service review, but only if we do not develop a reactive culture of blame.

Further reading

Alaszewski, H., Parker, A. & Alaszewski, A. (1999) *Empowerment and Protection: The development of policies and practices in risk assessmant and risk management in services for people with learning disabilities*. London: Mental Health Foundation.

Cambridge, P. (1997c) *HIV, Sex and Learning Disability*. Brighton: Pavilion.

Eby, M. (2000) The Challenges of Being Accountable. In: A. Brechin, H. Brown and M. Eby (Eds) *Critical Practice in Health and Social Care*. London: Sage.

Harris, J., Allen, D., Cornick, M., Jefferson, A. & Mills, R. (1996) *Physical Interventions: A policy framework*. Kidderminster: BILD.

References

Brown, H., Stein, J. & Turk, V. (1995) The sexual abuse of adults with learning disabilities: Report of a second two-year incidence survey. *Mental Handicap Research* **8** (1) 1–22.

Cambridge, P. (1996) Men with learning disabilities who have sex with men in public places: Mapping the needs of services and users in South East London. *Journal of Intellectual Disability Research* **40** (3) 241–251.

Cambridge, P. (1997a) How far to gay? The politics of HIV in learning disability. *Disability and Society* **12** (3) 427–453.

Cambridge, P. (1997b) At whose risk? Priorities and conflicts for policy development in HIV and intellectual disability. *Journal of Applied Research in Intellectual Disability* **10** (2) 83–104.

Cambridge, P. (1999) Considerations for informing safer sex education work with men with learning disabilities. *British Journal of Learning Disabilities* **27** (4) 123–126.

Cambridge, P. & McCarthy, M. (1997) Developing and implementing sexuality policy for a learning disability provider service. *Health and Social Care in the Community* **5** (4) 227–236.

Carson, D. (1990) Taking Risks with Patients – Your Assessment Strategy. In: *Professional Nurse: The Staff Nurse's Survival Guide*, pp83–87. London: Austen Cornish.

Fruin, D. (1998) *Moving into the Mainstream: The report of a aational inspection of services for adults with learning disabilities*. London: Department of Health.

Gunn, M. (1997) The Law, HIV and People with Learning Disabilities. In: P. Cambridge and H. Brown (Eds) *HIV and Learning Disability*. Kidderminster: British Institute of Learning Disabilities.

Horizon (1996) *Policy on HIV Infection and Testing for People with Learning Disabilities*. Abbots Langley: Horizon NHS Trust.

Jay, P. (1979) *Report of the Committee of Inquiry into Mental Handicap Nursing and Care*. London: HMSO.

McCarthy, M. (1997) HIV and Heterosexual Sex. In: P. Cambridge and H. Brown (Eds) *HIV and Learning Disability*. Kidderminster: BILD.

McCarthy, M. & Thompson, D. (1997) A prevalence study of sexual abuse of adults with intellectual disability referred for sex education. *Journal of Applied Research in Intellectual Disability* **10** (2) 105–124.

Thompson, D. (1997) Safer Sex Work with Men with Learning Disabilities Who Have Sex with Men. In: P. Cambridge and H. Brown (Eds) *HIV and Learning Disability*. Kidderminster: British Institute of Learning Disabilities.

 Part Two

KEY SKILLS

WRITTEN BY
Karen Bunning and
Nicola Grove

Chapter 6

Making Connections

KEY WORDS

communication
partner

communication
environment

a communication
ramp

exchange/
transactions

interaction,
interactive

non-verbal
behaviours

transaction

vocalisation

vulnerable
communication
areas

Understanding and promoting communication

Whoever you are, communication is a very complex process. We use the word, communication, to describe the messages (which we also call transactions or exchanges) that pass between two or more people. Communication is about the exchange of messages and also about building those messages into a relationship.

The people involved in every communication form a kind of partnership – both are working for the same thing, to ensure that their partner understands them. As communication partners, we build messages and meanings between ourselves and the person communicating with us (Grove *et al*, 2000).

We communicate meanings and ideas in many different ways: through **formal linguistic code** (ie language) including:

■ speech; writing; and sign and symbol (eg Makaton)

and through a range of **non-verbal behaviours** including:

- gesture; body language; eye gaze; and vocalisation – making sounds which aren't words.

Understanding the communication process

We can think of communication in terms of a series of circles, or levels (see **Figure 1,** below). There are several different elements that you need to consider when you are trying to communicate with an adult with a learning disability, three 'levels of influence'.

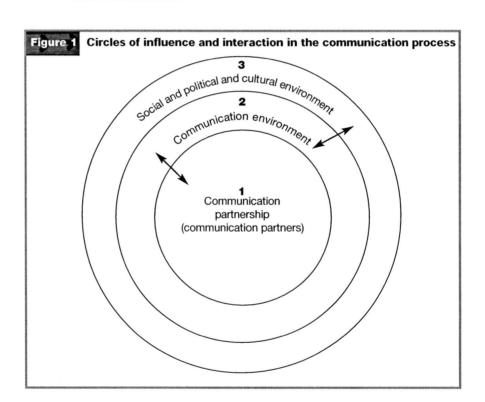

Figure 1 Circles of influence and interaction in the communication process

3
Social and political and cultural environment

2
Communication environment

1
Communication partnership
(communication partners)

1 **The communication partnership:**
   - the individuals' available communication skill set; experience; expectations and knowledge of partner(s) and context(s)

2 **The communication environment:**
- goals and values; service culture; philosophical interpretation

3 **The social and political and cultural environment:**
- beliefs and values; statutes and policies

How we treat people on a personal level (1 – the inner circle) and at the service level (2) can influence the way society (3) treats people. Equally, how society views people can influence how we treat people at a personal level. All three circles/levels of influence affect each other. They 'interact'.

For communication to be effective, it is important that there is a balance between all three levels. When one level exerts too strong an influence, you have an **imbalance**, and that causes problems – perhaps one level is ignoring some of the information at other levels.

We need to look at each level individually.

1 The communication partnership

At the most immediate level, you have two or more people together, trying to communicate, to pass messages between each other. Let's imagine you are trying to communicate with one other person. You and the other individual will both have various skills and experience that can help or hinder how successful you are at exchanging the information that you want to.

■ You may have certain personal or professional skills that will help – perhaps you can both speak English, perhaps you or your partner has a very open manner which makes the other person feel relaxed; perhaps you can use sign language which will help you to communicate.

- You might have known each other for a long time, and be familiar with each other's interests, moods and preferences. This personal knowledge/acquaintance may mean you can anticipate how and when the other person communicates best, as well as what they are trying to 'say'.

- You might have a lot of experience in communicating in creative ways. If you have been working with people with learning disabilities for a long time, in various settings, for example, you may have more ideas about different ways you can assist people to communicate. That is, you have some practice in interpreting what people's behaviour might or does mean, and you are able to apply this experience to a new 'partner', to a new situation.

All these things will affect how effective your interaction/exchange is, how well you understand each other.

Each person has different communication skills, and some people of course are more 'skilful' than others. It is important that we take others' personal levels of skills into account when we communicate with them, and adapt to their abilities. There may be problems for one or both of the people if neither adapts their skills to take into account the needs of their communication partner (Bartlett & Bunning, 1997). See **Example** opposite.

Encouragement and support

Because communication is interactive – that is, it relies on two or more people and their compatibility – our 'style' of communication can influence the ways in which the person with a learning disability is **seen** to communicate.

Communication partners may promote and encourage the skills of the service user. Alternatively, they may cast doubt on the abilities of the individual (Simmons-Mackie & Kagan, 1999).

Example

Jenny has a learning disability and communicates by making shapes with her hands (gestures), focusing her eyes on you (eye gaze), and making short grunting noises (vocalisation). Anna, the communication partner, uses conventional speech. Jenny and Anna communicate at different levels and there is a *difference* in their communication skills. This can lead to difficulties. This **unevenness/imbalance in their communication exchange may lead to**:

- **a struggle to express** ideas and feelings or to understand what is being communicated, which may lead to…

- **a breakdown in communication** where there is failure to exchange ideas, which may lead to…

- **disempowerment**, where the adult with a learning disability does not participate using available skills, which may lead to…

- feelings of **low self-esteem** and **frustration**, which may lead to…

- inappropriate ways of responding and behaviour that **challenges**, and results in…

- **isolation** and **social exclusion**.

When someone has communication difficulties, it is important that we make a more deliberate and focused input into any interaction. Using a typical conversational style of interaction may be completely ineffective. We need to develop **communication strategies** which are tailored to meet the communication needs of the person with a disability, ways of communicating which are most comfortable for them, not just us.

Adapting to others' needs

As carer, or friend, we must make conscious and consistent changes to the ways we offer communication support.

'…the most essential aspect of any attempt at communication is that it is presented in the way that is most likely to be understood…we need to explore alternatives and those alternatives are wide-ranging. We need to look at the whole repertoire of a person's body and facial language, how they move, and the sounds they make. Even if the language consists of incidental grunts, or clicks which are non-intentional, these may relate to activities which the person enjoys.'

Caldwell, 2000 (*You Don't Know What It's Like*)

The onus is on us to adapt to *their* needs and abilities, not the other way around. We must start from *their* point of view, rather than our own, and make efforts to meet them half way (or further than half way!) between our interpretation of the world and theirs.

This should allow the person with a disability to become more involved in the communication exchanged. If we do not do this, we do not help to bring out the best and clearest message from the individual.

It is helpful to think of times when this has happened to us, in an interaction that we have had with someone. We can all think of people and situations which have affected our ability to show what we know we can do, eg during an interview, or a conflict.

Where a person has communication difficulties, greater responsibility for the success or failure of the communicative act lies with the communication partner. If we are sensitive and responsive, the person with a disability may be able to demonstrate more skills. If we are hesitant and unsure, fail to recognise communicative signals or dominate an interaction with our own words, the person's skills will remain hidden.

2 The communication environment

Where your communication takes place – the communication environment – has a very strong influence on how successful your interaction is.

It is important to take into account various elements, including:

- **physical factors**, such as whether you are in a quiet enough room to hear or focus on small sounds, whether there are resources to help you communicate, such as pictures or lights, and so on

- **philosophical factors** ie wider considerations, the culture of the service you work in, what the service beliefs are, what is stated and encouraged as important in the care provided. For example, does the service encourage and value inclusion (both generally, and in terms of communication)? People need to be given the opportunity to communicate; does the service provide appropriate support, resources, time and so on?

 Opportunities to communicate and participate are strongly influenced by the culture of a service and its philosophical interpretation of service-user needs. In your service, are communication needs recognised and responded to, or is there a general view that you should communicate with everyone in the same way, regardless of their individual skills and needs?

When a communication environment fails to acknowledge and meet the individual needs of service users, it is likely that that service user's sense of control over themselves and their lives is threatened. They are disempowered by our attitude and actions (Bradshaw, 1998). Those individual needs may include hearing, vision and motor difficulties, psychosocial problems and cultural identity.

Example

Mohammed has no functional speech and communicates mainly through manual signs and gestures. The manager of the day centre he attends, however, feels that signing makes people with learning disabilities look odd and stand out in the community. She discourages their use, and has not learnt to sign herself. Mohammed arrives one morning and signs to the manager, 'It's cold!'. The manager's response is to tell him to stop flapping his hands around and take his coat off.

Setting up an effective and inclusive communication environment

There are many things which are taken into account in establishing an effective and inclusive communication environment. These include:

1 Setting

It's important to pay ongoing attention to variables that affect communication – the level of background noise, lighting, group size, for example – which must be considered in the context of service-user needs. Any essential adaptations should be carried out, such as providing a flashing-light fire alarm for those with a hearing impairment.

2 Values

It is important that the beliefs and goals of an organisation (ethos and policy statement etc) are generally known, and interpreted properly; this will have a positive effect.

For example: a total communication policy may prompt the integrated use of a range of communication strategies, including signs, gestures, body language, objects of reference (eg a favourite possession, or photograph) and symbols. Conversely, 'age-appropriateness' (speaking to an adult like an adult, and to a child like a child etc) may be given as a reason why people sometimes talk to the person with a learning disability by using a relaxed, 'conversational' style of interaction rather than adapting their communication to the needs of the person.

3   Skilful communication

Our knowledge and practical skills are critical to a supportive communication environment. These skills will help us to provide 'communication ramps'/aids for service users, such as the ability to modify our language, use signs, use strategies for people with hearing difficulties, touch, movement, etc.

4   Opportunities

The opportunities for participation that are usually provided in the communication environment should be structured to enable service users to show their communication strengths.

For example: achieving a balance in residents' meetings may be helped by the provision of a communication ramp in the form of a pictorial agenda.

These are all practical ways of improving the level of encouragement and support available to service users.

3 The social and political and cultural environment

The third 'circle'/level is the social and political environment, and involves the relationship between the service culture and provision and the wider society, the transition from one culture to another. The third 'level' encompasses the views and ethics of the community beyond your service.

- How does your society or culture see people with learning disabilities?

- Does your government provide resources and services to support them?

- What laws are in place to protect and help people with learning disabilities to live full lives?

- How does your personal or service view of, and relationship with, people with learning disabilities, conflict with society's view?

Conflicting perspectives

The third circle describes the move from an individual's participation in services (eg in groups, centres, consultation processes), to their participation in a range of opportunities in the community at large (eg taking part in non-service led activities). The latter may place rather more demands on an individual's communication skills.

This difference in perspectives can cause problems at the personal and service level as well. **For example:** if a society's or service's beliefs about what a person can do are different from what that individual *actually* can do, you have an imbalance. Perhaps a service believes strongly that an individual '*does not communicate*'? This can mean that if an individual *does* try to communicate, using sounds or gestures for example, the people around them won't recognise that that is what they are doing.

To counter these societal or service assumptions about what an individual can or cannot do, people with learning disabilities need to 'speak out'. **Political advocacy** describes the process whereby the views of service users are made known to those people who contribute to the broader political and social agenda.

Summary   This chapter has explored communication at three different levels of transaction:

1 The communication partnership

2 The communication environment

3 The social and political and cultural environment.

Communication with people with learning disabilities can easily break down. It is essential that we respond to service users' needs in a sensitive way, and that our approach to care and support involves the deliberate use of a broad spectrum of communication skills.

Further reading

Bartlett, C. & Bunning, K. (1997) The importance of communication partnerships: a study to investigate the communicative exchanges between staff and adults with learning disabilities. *British Journal of Learning Disabilities* **25** 148–153.

Bradshaw, J. (1998) Assessing and intervening in the communication environment. *British Journal of Learning Disabilities* **26** 62–66.

Foundation for People with Learning Disabilities (2000) *Choice Discovered.* A video and training materials. London: FPLD

Rondal, J. & Edwards, S. (1997) *Language in Mental Retardation.* London: Whurr.

References

Caldwell, P. (1998) *Person to Person.* Brighton: Pavilion.

Caldwell, P. (2000) *You Don't Know What It's Like.* Brighton: Pavilion.

Grove, N., Bunning, K., Porter, J. & Morgan, M. (2000) S*ee What I Mean: Guidelines to aid understanding of communication by people with severe and profound learning disabilities.* London: BILD & Mencap.

Grove, N., Bunning, K., Porter, J. & Olsson, C. (1999) See what I mean: Interpreting the meaning of communication by people with severe and profound intellectual disabilities. *Journal of Applied Research in Intellectual Disabilities* **12** 190–203.

Light, J. (1989) Towards a definition of communicative competence for individuals using augmentative and alternative communication systems. *Augmentative and Alternative Communication* **5** 137–144.

McConkey, R., Purcell, M. & Morris, I. (1999) Staff perceptions of communication with a partner who is intellectually disabled. *Journal of Applied Research in Intellectual Disabilities* **12** (3) 204–210.

Purcell, M., McConkey, R. & Morris, I. (2000) Staff communication with people with intellectual disabilities: The impact of a work-based training programme. *International Journal of Language and Communication Disorders* **35** 147–158.

Simmons-Mackie, N. & Kagan, A. (1999) Communication strategies used by 'good' versus 'poor' speaking partners of individuals with aphasia. *Aphasiology* **13** (9–11) 807–820.

WRITTEN BY
Steven Carnaby

Chapter 7

MAKING PLANS

KEY WORDS

person-centred

assessment

evaluation

planning

implementation

Undertaking assessment and care planning

We often take the day-to-day running of our lives for granted. Some of the things we do are almost automatic – getting out of bed in the morning, getting dressed, finding the cereal packet – while other activities, such as going on holiday, are likely to need more thought. This process of thinking about what we want or need to do involves weighing up the situation (*'Where do I want to go on holiday?' 'How long shall I go for?'*) and then some planning as to how things will happen (*'I'll cancel the milk, book a taxi to the airport and order some travellers' cheques'*).

People with learning disabilities are no different. They also need to assess the situation and plan before they act, and might need help to do this. In addition, it is possible that the *range* of activities needing assessment and planning will be greater, as people with learning disabilities often need some degree of support to get on with their lives. Indeed, using the example above, individuals with greater levels of disability might need a careful process of assessment and planning to help them to get out of bed and have breakfast, as well as for going on holiday.

'Good' support for people with learning disabilities needs careful planning if it is to meet an individual's needs appropriately, and therefore, skills in assessment and care planning are central to developing quality services. This chapter defines the assessment and care planning process, and suggests key elements for best practice in this important area.

Why are assessment and care planning so important?

Assessment and care planning form half of what can be described as 'the basic helping cycle' (Taylor & Devine, 1993), the other elements being implementation and evaluation. In practice, these four stages can be thought of as:

- *'What is the problem? What needs to be learnt? What are the strengths and limitations in this situation?'* (**assessment**)

- *'What should be done about it? By whom?'* (**planning**)

- *'Let's get into action!'* (**implementation**)

- *'How are things at the finish of our efforts?'* (**evaluation**)

It is useful to think of these elements as a cycle that is theoretically continuous (see **Figure 1**, below).

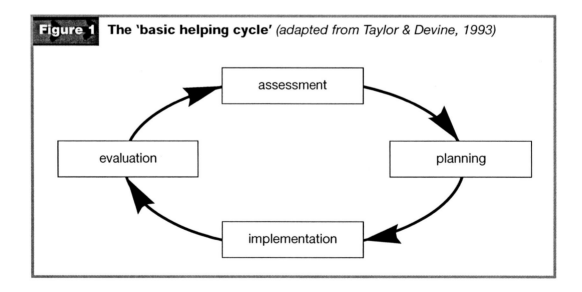

Figure 1 **The 'basic helping cycle'** *(adapted from Taylor & Devine, 1993)*

Assessment and planning are crucial – without these stages, the supporter is likely to 'dive in' and support the individual with learning disabilities without thinking about such important aspects as, for example:

- the extent and nature of what is needed

- potential risks

- how to be sure that the support provided is effective in meeting the individual's needs

- and most importantly, how to ensure the individual is fully involved in whatever is decided.

What is meant by 'assessment'?

Assessment is the process by which needs are identified, an aid for planning support or intervention. The characteristics of assessment are listed in **Box 1** (overleaf).

When using any assessment process, it is important to be clear about its **aims**. In practice this will mean that you need to:

1 establish the reason for undertaking the assessment

2 be clear about who will act on the information provided by the assessment

3 set out clear specific questions that you hope to answer using the information gathered in the assessment.

In other words, before undertaking an assessment of any kind, you should be able to answer the questions listed in **Box 2** (overleaf).

Box 1: Key characteristics of assessment

- Gathering information about the situation from as many sources as possible, but particularly from the perspective of the individual with learning disabilities

- Identifying potential areas for development or change as well as areas of strength and resourcefulness in the individual

- Placing the information gathered within specific relevant contexts eg frameworks relating to legislation, service policy, culture and ethnicity

- Identifying potential obstacles to any future work that may be carried out

- Establishing the level of existing strengths and needs as a baseline by which to measure progress of any future intervention

- Building strong rapport between the individual with learning disabilities and the individual(s) offering support, to encourage an open working relationship

 Box 2: Pre-assessment checklist

- Why is this question being asked?

- How will the information gathered be used?

- Who will use the information?

- Are the results of the assessment likely to be of practical benefit to the individual with learning disabilities?

If any of the answers to those questions is not straightforward, there is a good chance that you need to think more carefully about the type of assessment you have chosen.

The process of assessment

The precise nature of any assessment will clearly be linked directly with the individual, his or her situation and the issue(s) being addressed. However, assessments should always be:

- **reliable** – they could be repeated and similar outcomes would be achieved
- **efficient** – the outcome is worth the effort made
- **valid** – they give an accurate picture of what is happening
- **useful** – they fulfil a purpose.

The assessment process can be divided into the two main phases of:

1 gathering information

2 analysing information.

Gathering information

Information can be obtained in a variety of ways, including observation, interviewing the service user and his/her family, and using written sources. The precise strategy adopted would depend upon both the nature of the issue being addressed and the abilities and characteristics of the individual with learning disabilities you are supporting. The process will need to be adapted accordingly. For example, if the individual does not communicate in standard ways, your assessment could include creative techniques for ensuring that his/her perspective remains central to your findings. These techniques may include using video to record how the person shows others likes and dislikes, or supporting him/her to use a diary with photographs of activities.

Interviewing individuals with learning disabilities as part of your assessment

Where the individual *can* be interviewed more conventionally it is important that, as an interviewer, you are aware of the difficulties that have the potential to colour the information that you are recording. A wide body of research has suggested that interviews with people who have learning disabilities need to be conducted with a range of issues in mind. These are listed in **Box 3** (opposite).

Conducting observation

It may be helpful to conduct observations across a variety of settings and situations with the individual, alone and in a group. Observations should be planned and carried out with the individual's consent wherever possible, or with consent gained from significant others. It is important to record what you observe as objectively as possible, being aware of the context in which the events are occurring. Devise individualised recording sheets that capture the breadth and depth of information required.

Figure 1 (see page 102) shows an example of a simple observation sheet for recording incidences of challenging behaviour.

Other sources of information

Quite often, your assessment will form part of a wider multidisciplinary assessment, involving a range of professionals. It is essential that information is co-ordinated effectively through regular liaison. Sometimes, community team members, such as clinical psychologists and speech and language therapists, will conduct standardised assessments designed to assess specific abilities or phenomena.

Box 3:

Good practice in interviewing people with learning disabilities *(adapted from Ambalu, 1997)*

- Explain the purpose of the interview.
- If you are not familiar with the person, find out from carers or relatives the best way to communicate with him/her.
- Use short, simple sentences.
- Speak slowly.
- Pause after each sentence.
- Avoid the use of jargon.
- After making a statement, ask the person to tell you what you have said to check what they have understood.
- Use the person's communication aid(s) where appropriate.
- Break explanations down into steps and use photographs and/or drawings, if possible.
- Use open questions (for example 'tell me about…').
- Avoid using questions that require a yes/no answer.
- Be aware of difficulties in understanding time and number concepts (for example 'before' and 'after').
- If the person's speech is difficult to understand, do not pretend you have understood. Ask him or her to say it again/say it more slowly/say it in different words/show you what s/he means.
- Watch the person carefully to check that s/he is not becoming distressed.
- Remember that parents' or carers' views may differ from those of the person with learning disabilities.
- Sum up at the end of the session what will happen next.

Figure 1 Example of sheet for recording used during observation			
Date + Setting	What happened before the incident? (eg Who was around What was the person doing?)	Describe the incident (give as much detail as possible)	How did staff respond? (What did they say? What did they do?)

For example: the Wechsler Adult Intelligence Scale (WAIS 3rd edition) provides an assessment of an individual's cognitive abilities, whilst the Pre-Verbal Communication Scale (PVCS) establishes the individual's communication skills. Data gathered during interviews and observation provides invaluable context for the findings derived from these more standardised approaches.

Analysing information

The process of care planning

During assessment, information about the individual with learning disabilities and some aspect of his/her life is recorded and classified in some way. This information is analysed using your experience, knowledge and values, as well as that of your colleagues, and considered in the light of evidence from relevant research. Once a clear picture has been developed, planning for how to address the issue(s) can begin.

As with the assessment phase, it is essential that care planning is conducted with, and not just for, the individual with learning disabilities (and his/her family where appropriate). Care planning can be considered in terms of issues relating to the individual with learning disabilities and their family, issues concerning support staff and issues that relate to the wider support organisation. It is important that care planning remains **person-centred** in its approach and does not let organisational concerns and priorities make the individual's involvement in decision-making seem less important.

The structure of care planning

The term 'care planning' will mean slightly different things according to the organisation you work in. Care plans can refer to daily support plans providing details of how the person needs to be supported in daily activities (sometimes called 'support plans'), or can provide a much broader picture of the specific aspects of provision that combine to create a 'care package'. These are planning 'systems' that are given various names – eg Essential Lifestyle Planning; Pathways; Life Planning – but all aim to implement the ideology of a service organisation and support an individual to live as independently as possible and fulfil their potential in the community.

Clearly, the issue here is consistency of terminology and approach. The recent government white paper, *Valuing People*, advocates the use of planning that is person-centred as the backbone of effective provision for people with learning disabilities.

'A person-centred approach to planning means that planning should start with the individual (not with services) and take account of their wishes and aspirations. Person-centred planning is a mechanism for reflecting the needs and preferences of a person with a learning disability and covers such issues as housing, education, employment and leisure.'

Department of Health, 2001

Care plans can relate to a specific issue (eg intimate care or support with eating) or describe the ways in which an individual's lifestyle is supported more generally (eg making sure the individual has one-to-one support during the day). Whatever the nature or purpose of the care plan, the essential characteristic must be that it is person-centred, both in the process of its creation and during its implementation.

Main elements   Any care plan, whatever its scope, is likely to have the following elements:

- **Aims and objectives** (*What* are you and the individual trying to do and why?)

- **Methods** (*How* will you and the individual carry out the aims and objectives?)

- **Resources** (*Who/what* else will help? What materials, equipment or facilities might be needed?)

- **Timescale** (*How long* will the plan take to put into practice? Will it be broken down into smaller steps?)

- **Monitoring method** (How will you and the individual *record* what has been achieved?)

- **Evaluation method** (How will you know when stages of the plan have been achieved?)

The plan needs to be written down, but in ways that are primarily **meaningful to the individual with learning disabilities**. As with the assessment process, it is important to be creative and think laterally. Care plans can be recorded using video, photographs, symbols and signs, audiotape, drawings and interactive information technology (eg touch screen computers).

Care plan review

An equally vital stage of care planning is its review. This can be done in meetings involving people who have contributed to the plan's implementation. Again, involving the individual with learning disabilities must remain central. Historically, people with learning disabilities have been largely **excluded** from decision-making in *their* lives, and any attempts at care planning needs to avoid inappropriate meetings that are led by professionals and serve the needs of the organisation *before* the needs of the individual and his or her family. **Good practice in care planning review starts with the person and his/her ways of communication, and finds ways of integrating the person's views with concerns that the service may have regarding important issues, such as risk management and adult protection.**

Summary: Good practice in assessment and care planning

This chapter has attempted to describe the main characteristics of assessment and care planning and suggested some ideas for good practice. **Box 4** (overleaf) provides a summary checklist to get you started.

Box 4:
Checklist for good practice in assessment and care planning

- Start with the person and keep him or her at the centre of any assessment, planning or decision-making process.

- Consider the issue(s) you are addressing within the wider context of the individual's lifestyle and cultural background.

- Collaboration is essential – with the individual, with his or her social network and with other professionals within your organisation.

- Always base your assessment and planning on evidence from research.

- Be creative with how you support the individual with learning disabilities to express their views.

- Keep clear, concise records – and think carefully about who needs to know the outcomes of your assessment. Maintain confidentiality.

- Review the care plan regularly.

- Avoid making the individual feel as though s/he is living in a laboratory – remember that, within the complexities of charts, guidelines and observations, there lies a human being who should be respected and treated with dignity.

Further reading

Galambos, D. (1996) *Planning…To Have a Life: Individualised planning for quality of life*. Ontario, Canada: Sheridan College Learning Materials Service.

Sanderson, H. (1998) Person Centred Planning. In: P. Lacey. and C. Ouvray (Eds) *People with Profound and Multiple Learning Disabilities: A collaborative approach to meeting complex needs*. London: David Fulton.

Taylor, B. & Devine, T. (1993) *Assessing Needs and Planning Care in Social Work*. Aldershot: Arena.

Whittaker, A. (1993) Involving People with Learning Difficulties in Meetings. In: J. Bornat, C. Pereira, D. Pilgrim and F. Williams (Eds) *Community Care: A reader*. London: Macmillan.

WRITTEN BY
Peter McGill

Chapter 8

WHOSE LIFE IS IT ANYWAY?

KEY WORDS

accuracy and
appropriateness

confidentiality

communication

duty of care

data protection

negligence

ownership of
information

service-user
involvement

*Handling information
and keeping records*

In this, the information age, many of us would still rather 'have a go' than follow instructions, do something else rather than record what we've just done. Surely it's better, I hear you say, that we spend more time with the people we're supporting and less time in the 'office', reading and writing in files? These are natural instincts and, most of the time, will do no harm. But 'most of the time' is not good enough. Imagine you're receiving care in

hospital and the nurse does not read your file (which is stamped clearly, *allergic to penicillin*) and, by administering penicillin in accordance with the doctor's instructions (who also hasn't read your file), induces a severe allergic reaction. Such staff would be negligent and would have no defence against your complaint.

Similarly, if you, by not reading something you should have read or by not keeping an accurate record, cause harm to come to a person with learning disabilities, *you* are negligent in your duty of care. We may get away with it when we're assembling a new piece of furniture, but the use and accurate recording of information are not optional when we're working with people.

Furthermore, it's particularly crucial in work with people with learning disabilities. If you are conscious enough to see the nurse approaching you with a syringe, you may be able to ask what's in it… In a similar situation, many people with learning disabilities will not be able to do this or will not understand the implications of the answer (see **Box 1**).

 Box 1: Why we need to keep records

'This perspective inevitably leads to a concern with the procedures used for "remembering" the lives of people who cannot remember them for themselves. Since services cannot rely on the service user to tell them about the past and, partly because of staff turnover, cannot count on the memory of the staff, they need to provide a prosthetic memory through regular information collection… Record keeping, while undoubtedly often a boring chore, may need to assume a new importance as a method of helping to achieve personal and cultural continuity.'

Mansell *et al*, 2001

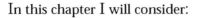

In this chapter I will consider:

- what information should be recorded

- how the information should be recorded – so that it is
  accurate and understood easily by those who need to use it

- how the information should be stored so that it is both
  secure and accessible

- the importance of confidentiality

- the legal context of 'data protection'

- how we can ensure as much service-user involvement as
  possible, including, where necessary, by the use of 'translation'
  services.

What information? Scepticism about the value of recording is often justified. In many services, far too much irrelevant information is recorded (and never used) so that staff can easily begin to feel that all recording is a waste of time. The first principle of handling information, therefore, is **not to create unnecessary information**. Records are much more likely to be kept (and used) if they have a **clear rationale** and can be completed quickly and easily. We'll use the example of Mrs E (see **Box 2**) to illustrate this.

> **Box 2: Mrs E**
>
> Mrs E was 70 and living in a house, with three others, supported by a small team of staff 24 hours a day (including sleep-in at night). She was an able lady who had spent a considerable period of time in a long-stay hospital, having been admitted at a time when it was enough to show unusual behaviour coupled with difficulty learning to read and write. Over the last few months her behaviour had become a cause of concern. She would often get up at night and stand at the top of the stairs, shouting about how her brother was dead. This usually woke up the member of staff and the other residents of the house, and it would often take some time to calm her down and for everyone to get back to sleep. Mrs E's brother was not dead and she spoke to him regularly on the phone.

What should we record here? First, we need to establish why we are recording. There are a number of possible reasons:

■ We may want Mrs E to see a psychiatrist or psychologist and think it will be helpful if we can say what has been happening, how often and how long it takes her to settle down.

- We may feel that having sleep-in cover is no longer sufficient for Mrs E and want to make a case to managers for temporarily having waking night staff.

- We may want to help Mrs E by checking out possible reasons for her getting upset and by checking out what strategies help her to calm down quickly.

Different reasons ought to lead to different recording strategies. We might decide that all these reasons are important and that we will seek to record the following:

- the time that Mrs E gets up and starts shouting

- what she shouts about

- the time she stops shouting and goes back to bed

- how long the sleep-in member of staff was awake (not just managing the situation, but also recording it!)

- whether other residents were disturbed and for how long

- whether anything happened the previous evening that might have upset Mrs E – we might already have suspicions about this and, if so, would seek to record this more specifically (eg whether Mrs E had spoken to her brother on the phone).

It's worth remembering again why this kind of recording is likely to be necessary. If and when Mrs E sees a psychiatrist, the latter is likely to want to know how long this has been happening for and how often. Even with her relatively good communication skills, Mrs E may not be able to say. If she is accompanied by a member of staff, that person may have some information but, without systematic recording, they will only be able to give a very partial account – what's happened on the one night a week when they have been sleeping in. Thus Mrs E is disadvantaged either by the psychiatrist making a decision on the basis of incomplete information or by delaying a decision until such information is gathered.

How to record The most common means of recording information is through some kind of 'diary' in which staff (and occasionally service users) write a narrative account of what has happened. Imagine such a diary entry for Mrs E:

'Up all night again with Mrs E screaming and shouting.
Mrs D got a bit upset too because she couldn't get back to sleep.
I can't cope with this much longer – is anyone doing anything?'

I expect we've all seen diary entries like this, though, of course, we've never made them ourselves! Diaries have many problems, for example:

- they often fail to separate fact from opinion

- they are often inaccurate (what does 'up all night' mean?)

- they often miss out important information (what was Mrs E shouting about?).

Such records are also very difficult to use. As the diary builds up over days and weeks, the amount of information grows to the point where it would take someone a considerable amount of time to 'mine' it for what is really important eg how many nights has Mrs E been upset and, on average, for how long?

Often, therefore, a more structured approach to record keeping will be better. Such records are usually much easier for staff to keep (they involve mainly ticking boxes rather than writing at length) and they are much, much easier to use and summarise – at a glance, for example, the member of staff coming in the next day can see what sort of a night Mrs E and the others have had. In Mrs E's case, a record form along the lines of that shown in **Table 1** (opposite) might be used.

Table 1 A sample recording form

Night	Start time	What Mrs E did (eg shouted about her brother being dead)	Stop time	What helped to calm her down (eg talked quietly to her)	Other residents disturbed?	Anything that upset Mrs E? (eg brother didn't phone previous evening)
Monday						
Tuesday						
Wednesday						
Thursday						
Friday						
Saturday						
Sunday						

Storing and retrieving information

There's nothing worse than spending a lot of time recording information and then not being able to find it when you need it. This happens to us all, of course – recording is second only to filing in many people's list of pet hates. But if you can't find it, you can't use it and you really have wasted your time. Worse, if you can't find it, that might mean it's been left somewhere it shouldn't have been (like on the dining room table) and is currently being read by someone who shouldn't read it. So storage of information is a vital part of the recording process – making sure that the information can then be accessed by those who need it… and only by those who need it. There are many different solutions to the storage/filing problem and it would not be appropriate to prescribe particular approaches here. But whatever system you use should meet the following criteria:

- It's easy for you to put information into it.
- It's easy for appropriate others to access that information.
- It's *not* easy for *in*appropriate others to access the information.

Confidentiality and data protection

Confidentiality requires that we *'respect the privacy of service users by taking responsible care of information gained during professional activity, and, in the absence of special circumstances, divulging it only with permission'* (Prince, 2000).

Most of us don't want our personal business talked about in public or displayed on the wall. People with learning disabilities are at much greater risk of breaches of their confidentiality because of living their lives in more 'public' circumstances. Such breaches are only justified where there is evidence that the person might be in danger (eg of abuse) should the information not be passed on. Concerns about confidentiality should not affect everyday working practices involving the sharing of information. Staff have a duty to work as part of a team and the sharing of information is part of this.

At times, information may be held back from staff on a 'need to know' basis, where it is thought that the sharing of the information might harm the person or their reputation significantly. This is often a tricky judgement. Staff should be given information that helps them to do their job in supporting service users but staff, like us all, are subject to prejudice and bias and may respond inappropriately to an individual because of some aspect of their history. Staff should certainly not be denied relevant information, however, where this would put their own or others' safety at risk.

The *Data Protection Act 1998* lays out eight principles. All data must be:

- processed fairly and lawfully

- obtained and used only for specified and lawful purposes

- adequate, relevant and not excessive

- accurate and, where necessary, kept up to date

- kept for no longer than necessary

- processed in accordance with the individual's rights

- kept secure

- transferred only to countries that offer adequate data protection.

These principles apply both to data recorded electronically and in paper form. Individuals have a general right of access to information held about them, though information may be withheld if it can be established that it would not be in the person's best interests to see it. The *Data Protection Act* imposes legal obligations on organisations but these obligations are primarily about following good practice. **One significant benefit is that the knowledge that the person, about whom we are writing, might read what we have written does tend to lead to a more respectful and objective approach to the recording of information.**

Involving service users
We must always remember that the reason we keep records and handle information in the ways described above is to benefit service users. *'Nothing about us without us'* means that we should always consider how the records we are keeping can be made accessible to people with learning disabilities and whether they can be involved in the record keeping process. There are a number of things to think about here:

■ Does the person know that records are being kept? Unless there is a very good reason they ought to know and be happy about it – imagine, for a moment, finding out by chance that someone has been keeping records about your bowel movements without telling you! – and ought, as far as possible, to understand why the records are being kept.

■ If the person objects to the records being kept you need to consider with your colleagues and manager what you should do. There are many circumstances in which you will decide that you need to keep a record anyway (eg because you have a duty of care to the person), but you should take their objections seriously and consider whether there are alternative, more acceptable ways of doing what you feel you need to do.

- Sometimes it will be more acceptable to the person if they are involved in the record-keeping process eg by ticking the boxes on your chart, or by keeping their own record. Service-user involvement will be much easier if the recording system is structured and simple to use. As is so often the case, making something accessible to a person with disabilities also makes it more accessible and easier to use for the person without disabilities.

- Service-user involvement will be considerably enhanced by presenting things in a 'language' they can understand. In some cases (eg the person brought up speaking Punjabi) this may mean employing a translator. In other cases it may mean ensuring that information is available in Braille, or Makaton symbols, or whatever the preferred mode of communication is for an individual. People who can't write or make marks are not restricted from keeping records eg a tape recorder may provide the means of an excellent and accessible record.

Summary Handling information is a central part of working with people with learning disabilities. Good practice involves:

- being clear about why we need the information

- collecting only the information we need

- making sure that we collect accurate information that can be easily used

© Pavilion, 2002

- storing information securely but making sure it is accessible to those who need it
- respecting confidentiality
- acting lawfully, in line with the *Data Protection Act*
- involving service users as much as possible.

Most importantly, good practice involves using the information that has been gathered and stored so that we, ourselves, act in ways that are consistent with the best information about a person's needs and that we are constantly striving to learn (from the records of our own and others' experience) how to do a better job.

References and further reading

Mansell, J., McGill, P. & Emerson, E. (2001) Development and evaluation of innovative residential services for people with severe intellectual disability and serious challenging behavior. *International Review of Research in Mental Retardation* **24** 245–298.

Prince, K. (1996) *Boring Records? Communication, speech and writing in social work.* London: Jessica Kingsley.

Prince, K. (2000) Confidentiality. In: M. Davies (Ed) *The Blackwell Encyclopaedia of Social Work* pp74–75. Oxford: Blackwell.

United Kingdom Central Council for Nursing, Midwifery and Health Visiting (1998) *Guidelines for Records and Record Keeping.* London: UKCCNMHV.

WRITTEN BY
Angela Cole
and Ann Lloyd

Chapter 9

IT'S NOT WHAT YOU KNOW, IT'S WHO!

KEY WORDS

community

connections

relationships

social inclusion

Enabling and supporting community involvement

What is it that makes you feel a part of a community? Any community – whether it's where you live, your work, sports club, political group, religious group, or one of the numerous other communities you probably relate to. Take a moment to think about it.

Done? Our bet is that you may have come up with words or phrases like *'friends'*, *'a sense of belonging'*, *'similar interests'*, *'shared beliefs and goals'*, *'common experiences'*, *'having fun together'*, *'knowing people'*, *'making a contribution that's valued'*. Most, if not all, will reflect some form of interaction and unity between you and other people – because, essentially, that's what feeling a part of a community is all about. Even the most modern communities – in cyberspace – are all about people interacting with each other.

So, if feeling part of a community – feeling involved – is about relationships and interaction, then a key task for people supporting citizens with learning difficulties has to be to deliberately build their connections with others. In this chapter we explore why building community connections and involvement is so crucial, and offer some ideas about how to go about it.

But, what does 'community' mean?

An important question! The King's Fund provided guidance in 1988:

'The best way we have found of thinking about community is to imagine it as the set of ties and connections which a person has with others.'

There's clearly a dilemma when thinking about people who spend a great deal of their time in segregated settings (like village communities, long-stay hospitals, day centres). Are we advocating that individuals be supported to build 'ties and connections' with other disabled people in segregated communities? In part, we are. At the personal level, having friends around us day-to-day enhances our lives. Disabled people have shared experiences and issues – a 'community of interest' – which is the basis for development of advocacy and pressure groups. Enabling people with learning difficulties to come together to enjoy each other's company and to gain strength from each other is positive and desirable. *But*, building community connections and involvement is, and must be, about more than that.

We have to look beyond the community of disabled people. If we don't, we fail people, we fail ourselves, and we fail society. In 1992, John O'Brien and Connie Lyle O'Brien wrote…

'…*exclusion decreases the human diversity that can energise civic life, with obvious cost to people with severe disabilities and their families*'.

It is fundamentally a moral issue about the kind of society we want to live in.

 'Segregation is the offspring of an illicit intercourse between injustice and immorality.'
Martin Luther King, Jr

Steve Dowson, exploring the meaning of community (1995), describes a '*personal community – a matrix of people, places, and roles, unique to each individual*' which '*provides not only a sense of identity for the person, but actual identity in the eyes of others*'. Thus, building connections *beyond* the community of disabled people gives people identity in society. It demonstrates people's status as citizens. It opens the door to more friendships, and to informal, natural support. But, as he points out, what is really important is that people are helped to build connections and involvement in their local area – with their neighbourhood community. It is interaction with local people that can give a real sense of belonging.

Supporting people to get involved in their neighbourhood community also recognises that people with learning difficulties have something to offer others.

Amitai Etzioni (2000) states that *'mutuality is central to communities. A good society relies even more on mutuality – people helping each other rather than merely helping those in need...'*

With citizenship rights go responsibilities. People with learning difficulties share a responsibility to contribute to the development of a 'good society'. Building ordinary community connections provides the opportunity for people to step out of a dependency role and give something to their local community and society.

Does involvement really matter? Isolation and loneliness are a big social problem, and it is clear from research that most people with learning difficulties have very limited social networks, making loneliness more likely (Bayley, 1997). Being an active participant in a number of communities makes life enjoyable and stimulating. *Feeling* involved and a part of things can help give us a sense of worth and purpose and, ultimately, it may help prevent mental health problems. Many people with learning difficulties have lives that revolve around the services they attend and their family. Their contact with local people is through, or mediated by, their parents or staff. They do not themselves have reciprocal relationships with people other than family. As their close family declines, they are in danger of becoming even more bereft of the warmth and joy that reciprocal relationships with others bring. It is essential that services recognise this and do things to help people build a range of relationships and connections *now*.

For people from ethnic minorities, involvement with their own cultural community can help to overcome feelings of difference, and fears of prejudice or rejection (Baxter *et al*, 1990).

For **Halil**, a Turkish Cypriot in London, one of the most important things about being supported to go to the gym every week is that he often sees a woman there who speaks Turkish with him. He loves going to a local café run by Turkish Cypriot people because he feels at home, but the community day service doesn't support him to go there often. He is disappointed that there are no staff supporting him who share his culture or language. Halil feels there is a gap in his life and wants to do more alongside other Turkish Cypriot people. Being involved with his own community really matters to him.

Yes! Being connected and involved with other people is important – it's what makes life worth living. Communities are about people, and the greater their – our – involvement and contribution, the more a community benefits.

So, how do we build people's connections and involvement? There is no single way! Take a flexible, multi-pronged approach. Throw lots of balls in the air – at least one may hit the target and a new connection flourish! Here are some ideas about approaches that can help.

■ Build circles of support

Assist someone to bring a group of people together to help improve their life and realise their goals and dreams. Help them identify people they have a close, reciprocal bond with, others they want to get to know better, or who show a genuine interest in them. If someone has limited networks, you may need to engineer and facilitate membership of their circle – laying the foundation for natural relationships to develop in the longer term.

■ Do things consciously and deliberately

For most of us, community connections and involvement develop naturally during the normal course of daily life. This does not necessarily happen for people with learning difficulties. So it is important to deliberately plan a course of action that aims to achieve that goal. This is one of the paradoxes of the work. You very often have to do something specially planned – something which might seem artificial – in order to achieve something natural. In this case, create new bonds of friendship between people.

■ Support people to be *in* the community

Being physically in the community makes it easier for people to develop their connections and involvement, so help people to live in ordinary homes in ordinary streets, use public facilities, get jobs, go to college – it's the best starting point. Lots of us make friends or start relationships, for example, through our work.

 There are three people at the heart of **Cathy**'s circle: her mum, her keyworker from the residential home where she lives, and a woman called Jenny. Cathy met Jenny through her work in an elderly person's home. They work alongside each other and have developed a close bond. Jenny rarely misses any of Cathy's circle meetings and they now exchange cards and gifts as well. With careful nurturing their friendship has the potential to grow and flourish beyond the workplace.

■ ...and then make sure it continues

Like us, you've probably come across many people who have ended their involvement in something they enjoyed, and consequently lost touch with people, because their service changed – their support worker left, a policy changed, money became tight, or they may have had to move away from their home. People's community connections and involvement are often at the mercy of the services and support they receive, and it is one of the greatest threats. Being conscious of this is the starting point; taking positive action to sustain people's involvement whilst all around them may be changing is the challenge.

Julie lives in Liverpool. Soon after leaving school she was supported to move from a special needs unit in a day centre to take up a youth training scheme work placement with the electricity board. She initially received on the job support from a supported employment worker, but eventually one of her work colleagues took over. She made a lot of new friends, and when there was a reorganisation at work, it was her colleagues who designed a new job for her so that she still had a role. On her 21st birthday Julie had a party packed with friends, family and workmates.

The policy was that youth training placements could only last two years, and at the end of that time Julie returned to the day centre. Involvement with her work friends tailed off. Julie went from being a 'workmate' to a 'service user', from an integrated community to a segregated one again. The benefits that Julie had got from youth training were not sustained.

■ Know the community

To develop connections and involvement you need to know about the community, whether a neighbourhood, a work community, or any other. Where do people pass the time of day? Who are the socialites, and where do people go to socialise? Who could do with some support? Who is interested in what? There are two options: either you get to know the community yourself, or you seek out someone in that community (for example, a key resident: the Dot Cotton of the street!) to help. The latter is particularly important where you are trying to build someone's connections with an ethnic minority community but you are not, yourself, from that community.

■ Do things that benefit the whole community

> *'What is not good for the hive is not good for the bee.'*
> Marcus Aurelius

Another way of thinking about this is that supporting someone to do something good for the community will also be good for the person in their own right. Taking a community development approach is about helping people with learning difficulties to contribute something for the benefit of all. It means finding out what the community is missing, or would like to have, and then taking the lead in developing it. For example, setting up a Local Exchange Trading Scheme would enable people to contribute to their neighbourhood community on an equal basis, at the same time as getting to know local people much better. Community development undertaken in partnership with other members of that community can forge connections and a shared purpose. It creates a sense of belonging. It is important, though, that it is the person with learning difficulties that gets the sense of belonging, not you. Any development must be about you supporting and facilitating, doing things with the person rather than taking over as their main link with other people.

One of the things that makes community involvement more difficult for people with learning difficulties, particularly if they have mobility problems, visual impairments or live in rural areas, is access to public buildings and good transport. But it can be a problem for so many other people too, like young parents with pushchairs and elderly people. Initiating or joining a campaign to improve community transport and access is just one example of action that might benefit the whole community.

■ Reflect on, and change, what you do

John and Connie O'Brien (1992) challenge staff and services to actively encourage community involvement, to prioritise people's relationships, contacts and memberships and organise flexibly around them. They challenge staff to be conscious of their own power:

'Service staff could reduce barriers…if they stopped acting as if they own the people they serve and could arbitrarily terminate their contacts or disrupt their memberships'.

Again, the requirement is to act consciously. Building community connections and involvement needs to be 'live' in your mind so that opportunities are recognised and grasped.

 Bola is a young black woman living in an area where mostly white people live. She has no friends who share her ethnic background. Bola was with Amy, a project worker, when they met another young black woman working at the office reception. It soon became clear that the woman recognised Bola from around the village, and they struck up a conversation. The woman finished the conversation by saying how nice it was to meet Bola and hopefully they would meet again. And that's how it was left. Later, Amy kicked herself for not having supported Bola to make an arrangement, there and then, to meet the woman again. It was now much more difficult to do, without her name, address or phone number.

■ Local, regular and targeted

It's not enough just to support people to be *in* the community. It's what you do there that makes the difference when it comes to achieving real involvement. Many day services, for example, arrange regular trips and 'outings' as part of their programme of activities. These '… *can give people a good experience but do little to build people's involvement in, or sense of belonging to their community*' (Lloyd & Cole, 2000). Doing things locally means that people are more likely to bump into each other beyond services and there's more chance they will build a connection.

 Jack, and a few others, are supported by their day service to go out for a pub lunch every Wednesday. They have been going to the same pub each week for many months, so they are now known by the staff and other regulars. Jack feels comfortable and at home in the pub.

It sounds like there's a good foundation to build on – until we consider that the pub is actually 35 miles away from where Jack and his friends live. They can't get there on their own, and the chances of them ever seeing people from the pub when they are not using the day service are very slim indeed!

© Pavilion, 2002

Going to the same local places, and doing the same activities regularly, like a weekly slimming group, running club, or evening class – where people share a goal or passion – is more likely to result in sustainable connections than going at *ad hoc* times.

Think carefully about the best places and circumstances for meeting people. It may not be the gym (a fairly solitary activity) unless there's also a bar or café where people tend to gather after their workout. Is it a place where people stay around with time to relax, or a more 'transitory' venue with people just passing through? Choose activities carefully with connections in mind. People are more likely to build links with others if they share something in common. It is essential that you know the person well – their interests, preferences, talents, worries. Then you can target your efforts on activities, places and people that have the potential to enhance the person's life. Don't forget that a lot of community life and networks revolve around children. Help people make links with families.

■ Support people to stay in touch

Supporting people to keep in touch with family, friends and new acquaintances can take effort, especially if people live a long way away. You may need to help someone make a phone call, send post cards, photos, birthday cards, invitations: small but important actions that oil the wheels of relationships.

 Jonathan moved back to his local area from hospital in the early '90s. He had no contact with his family, used a wheelchair, had little speech and little was known about his interests, likes or dislikes. He went out infrequently – hostel staff were anxious because he would scream and bang his head – until he was specifically linked to two support workers to go out with him on different days of the week.

Jonathan clearly liked being out, even in bad weather, but it was really hard to get a sense of other things he liked to do. 'Going out' was in danger of losing its purpose. The workers therefore visited the hospital to try to get some information about things he had done before or interests he may have had. The visit gave them few clues about his interests, but they did find out that Jonathan had a friend, Paul, who had moved back to the local area from hospital previously. The workers arranged for the two to meet up. It went well and Paul indicated that he'd like to see Jonathan regularly. Jonathan and Paul were helped to rekindle their friendship and then to develop a shared interest in tropical fish. Jonathan's life took a turn for the better.

■ Help the public to open the door

It's still very common to hear people saying that they 'couldn't' support people with learning difficulties, and that they admire people who do. The shame is that many members of the public have simply not been used to having people with learning difficulties participate alongside them. When it happens, people soon overcome their pre-conceived ideas and fears, begin to feel comfortable and grow in confidence. It is about familiarity and learning, leading to the development of what John McKnight calls '*authentic citizen communities of care*' (1995).

We have a role to play in helping members of the community build their confidence and capacity to welcome people with learning difficulties. It's about paving the way – a worker accompanying someone with their potential new friend so they gain confidence with each other, or working with staff in sports centres, cinemas, or clubs, so they gain an understanding of an individual with learning difficulties who will be joining them.

Stephen lives in an area where bowling is an important sport and social activity. He was really keen to join the bowling club in his village, but the club committee were concerned that he would not know how to play and would spoil other people's enjoyment. They said 'no'. A worker went to see the Chair of the committee and explained that Stephen just needed someone to teach him. As a result a couple came forward and said they would help Stephen. He was signed up as a member of the club and began to play bowls with them regularly.

■ Emphasise what people can contribute

Supporting people to take on a role – as a good neighbour, a loving uncle, a handy-person – helps others to see them as equal. It reinforces citizenship and makes a positive contribution to community life. It is easier to help someone get involved in a community if they are seen as having something to offer rather than as needing something.

 Ivan was clear that he wanted to get involved with a local drama group. He loves acting and has done some television work in the past. His parents are both in the business. People in Ivan's planning circle enthusiastically approached some local groups but found the initial responses very disappointing. People were close to giving up. The breakthrough came when people changed what they said when contacting a group. Instead of talking about Ivan's disability, they focused on what he could do to help the group – the talents he had to offer and the contribution he could make. Ivan joined a group, was soon written into their next production and rehearsing two evenings a week. He was over the moon and made several new contacts in his local community.

Contributing something may be about a person in a wheelchair lining up alongside local parents and older people to campaign for better access, or joining the horticultural society and growing vegetables on an allotment for the local farmers market. Someone with limited mobility and no speech can still hand out hymnbooks at a church service or smile a welcome to people attending a football supporters club meeting. There are so many different ways that people can contribute to their local community. We just need to focus on people's talents and gifts and use our creative and imaginative thinking.

Network, network, network

Building connections and involvement is partly about what you know and what you do, but it's also a lot about *who* you know and how you use your own, and other people's, networks. If you don't know anyone in the horticultural society, your neighbour might; if you don't know a regular supporter of the local football team, your milkman might. Don't be afraid to ask people for help and ideas. You might get a few rejections along the way, but you're more likely to get some good leads and new ideas.

It's about you and me

As John O'Brien wrote in 1989:

'Developing high quality human services…calls for reallocation of service resources, working outside traditional boundaries, and renegotiation of the service's position in community life. This essential work calls for the motivation arising from a vision of inclusive community…'

As ordinary citizens, we want to be involved with communities where people with learning difficulties have a place and take an active part. We want to run into people, as friends, at the library, the allotment, the bus-stop; we want to see people as colleagues at work, on committees, in action groups; we want to share experiences with people as students, worshippers, neighbours. We believe that inclusion strengthens communities and society and that we therefore have a responsibility, beyond our work, to do things that help achieve this.

Community inclusion is about what we do in our own lives. What do you do in yours?

This piece first appeared in Living WELL *(2000) Volume 1 Issue 1, published by Pavilion.*

Further reading

Dowson, S. (1995) What do we mean by 'community'? *Community Living* **8** (3) 6–7.

King's Fund (1988) *Ties and Connections: An ordinary community life for people with learning difficulties.* London: King's Fund.

Lloyd, A. & Cole, A. (2001) Building Positive Lifestyles: The community option. In: C. Clark (Ed) *Better Days: Adult Day Services and Social Exclusion.* London: Jessica Kingsley.

O'Brien, J. & O'Brien, C. L. (1992) Members of Each Other: Perspectives on social support for people with severe disabilities. In: J. Nisbet (Ed) *Natural Supports in School, at Work, and in the Community for People with Severe Disabilities.* Baltimore: Paul Brookes Publishing.

References

Bayley, M. (1997) *What Price Friendship?* Minehead: Hexagon Publishers.

Baxter, C., Poonia, K., Ward, L. & Nadirshaw, Z. (1990) *Double Discrimination: Issues and services for people with learning difficulties from black and ethnic minority communities.* London: King's Fund.

Etzioni, A. (2000) The road to the good society. *New Statesman* (May issue) pp25–27.

McKnight, J. L. (1995) *The Careless Society: Community and its counterfeits.* New York: Basic Books.

O'Brien, J. (1989) *What's Worth Working For? Leadership for better quality human services.* Lithonia, Georgia: Responsive Systems Associates.

Members of the High Spin dance company; a promotional shot for *The Surgeon's Waltz*.

Promotional shot from the *Rice Rain* tour, 2001.

WRITTEN BY
Hazel Morgan

Chapter 10

IT'S MY CHOICE

KEY WORDS

choice

advocacy

self-advocacy

peer advocacy

Understanding and promoting advocacy and decision-making

Choice: Lloyd Page, Vice Chair of Inclusion Europe, writes…

'Really very few people are so disabled that they can't make any choices, if they are given the opportunity.

'Choice is important to us; it may be a nuisance having to make our minds up, but it is a great deal better than having our minds made up by someone else… or other people pretending that we don't have a mind that we could make up.'

Foundation for People with Learning Disabilities, 2000

Background The right of people with learning disabilities to make choices has now been recognised by the Government. One of the objectives of the recent white paper *Valuing People* (2001) is:

'…to enable people with learning disabilities to have as much choice and control as possible over their lives through advocacy and a person-centred approach to planning the services and support they need.'

Some years ago, such a statement would have been unimaginable. People with learning disabilities were routinely denied choice. For those in long-stay hospitals, the choice about where they would live, what they would do each day, whom they would associate with, what they would wear and eat was decided for them.

Those living with families might have more choice, but nonetheless, many decisions would be made by other family members and opportunities would be restricted by the way services were organised. For example, it would be assumed that on leaving school the young person would go to an adult training centre or day centre.

For over a quarter of a century, the idea that people with learning disabilities should be empowered and enabled to take control of their lives has gradually gained ground. This has been brought about by various things...

- **The normalisation movement**, which originated in Scandinavia and the USA in the 1960s and early 1970s. This recognised the harm done to people living in large institutions and demanded that the lives of people with learning disabilities should be as close to normal living conditions as possible

- **The civil rights movement** which challenged the oppression experienced by many minority groups, including people with learning disabilities, and sought to remove barriers to playing a full part in society

- **The development of a social model of disability** (rather than a medical model), which emphasised the importance of removing these barriers to enable disabled people to be part of their communities

- **The growth of a self-advocacy movement**

- **Society** as a whole has placed more emphasis on individual choice

- O'Brien and Tyne (1981) formulated the **five service accomplishments**: community presence; choice; competence; respect and participation, which many agencies acknowledged as the values underpinning their services.

Problems with making choice a reality

It takes a long time to change attitudes and gain acceptance for the idea that people with learning disabilities can and should make choices. Although many agencies paid lip service to O'Brien's five service accomplishments, the reality was often that choice was limited, particularly if someone had a severe learning disability.

If there *is* to be choice, then opportunities need to be provided so that people can experience a range of options. Often people have led very restricted lives and need to be introduced gradually to choices.

140

'One way in which people learn about their own preferences and abilities is by trying out new experiences.'

Mental Health Foundation, 1996

- People need to be listened to and their choices respected. This demands time from staff and others to hear what people are saying and flexibility in services to accommodate choice and change.

- If people with learning disabilities use few or no words, then those close to them need to establish a way of communicating together, so that their preferences can be established.

- Some people will need support in making choices and in this respect the advocacy movement is very important.

- Care staff have a crucial role to play in enabling those they support to make choices.

The development of the advocacy movement

With the growing emphasis on rights and inclusion, an advocacy movement developed. The first group organised by people with learning disabilities in the USA was formed in Oregon in 1973 and was called People First. Similar groups were formed in Scandinavia in the early '70s.

The different kinds of advocacy

There are two main types of advocacy:

- **self-advocacy**, defined as people speaking up for themselves, and

- **citizen advocacy**, where citizen advocates (ie volunteers) create a relationship with a person with learning disabilities, seeking to understand and represent their views.

Self-advocacy

In **self-advocacy groups**, members give each other mutual support and usually have a facilitator to assist them. In addition to speaking up for themselves individually, the range of activities in which members have been involved have included:

- consciousness-raising sessions
- encouraging members to adopt new roles, such as involvement in staff selection
- campaigns to get rid of old terminology
- direct action, for example, to improve transport facilities for disabled people
- campaigns to change policy and the law
- promoting direct payments
- involvement in service planning
- involvement in research
- organising national and international conferences
- addressing the United Nations (Emerson *et al*, 2000).

Citizen advocacy

'Citizen advocacy is needed for people with severe learning disabilities because their access to services and other facilities may depend on their having someone to speak up on their behalf… citizen advocates are needed because others involved in the lives of people with learning disabilities are likely to have pressures on them which prevent them from being independent and objective.'

Brooke & Harris, 2000

In citizen advocacy, the focus is likely to be on the needs and wishes of the individual. There is a challenge still to be addressed in how to hear the voice of those with the most severe disabilities in the planning of services.

Other forms of advocacy include:

- peer advocacy
- short-term or crisis advocacy
- children's and youth advocacy.

Peer advocacy, where people with learning disabilities speak up on behalf of people with more severe learning disabilities, if it were to expand, might enable their views to be more clearly heard in the planning of services as well as providing a valuable voice for individuals.

Short-term or **crisis advocacy** is needed when someone has a particularly pressing issue such as a place to live or a serious medical problem. If the person has a severe disability it is important that they know the person already, to be sure they are conveying their wishes.

Children's and youth advocacy has not been widely developed, but could have an important role to play in raising the consciousness of young people with regard to their rights and opportunities.

Problems in the development of the advocacy movement

Often, the development of the movement in England has been hampered by inadequate and/or time-limited funding. Some groups are dependent on bodies such as charitable trusts. Others receive grants from local authorities or health trusts. This in its turn can create problems. It is important that groups are independent of services. Other issues to bear in mind include:

- It is often hard to recruit and retain sufficient volunteers.
- Sections 1 and 2 of the *Disabled Persons Act 1986* would have provided everyone with the right to an advocate and required the development of an independent advocacy service by every authority, but they have never been implemented.

- The movement has remained fragmentary and vulnerable.

- Advocates have not always been recognised.

 The (Pathways to Citizen Advocacy) project heard a number of accounts where citizen advocates were denied access to residential homes or day centres, or refused information relating to major concerns about their partner. There were also instances of advocates being ignored by service commissioners or providers – or even told outright that as advocates they had no standing.

Foundation for People with Learning Disabilities, 2000

The relationship of the advocate with others

It is clear that the wishes of the self-advocate should be paramount. For people with learning disabilities in an advocacy partnership, there will be other people who are also close to them, such as the keyworker, care staff, family and friends. There will need to be respect for one another and sensitivity to the different roles that people play in the life of the person with learning disabilities, to ensure that their voice is truly heard.

Challenges for the future

The white paper, *Valuing People*, described a key challenge for services in England and Wales, as the setting up of…

'…*a range of independent advocacy services in each area so that people with learning disabilities can choose the one which best meets their needs.*'

It has set aside £1.3 million for each of the three years, 2001–2004. This money is intended to:

- establish a **National Citizen Advocacy Network** led by a consortium of leading voluntary organisations

  - This consortium will be charged with distributing funds to local groups in an equitable and open manner. The funding is not to be used to replace existing funding sources for citizen advocacy. The British Institute of Learning Disabilities (BILD) has been commissioned by the Department of Health to play the leading role.

- **increase funding** for local self-advocacy groups and strengthen the national infrastructure for self-advocacy

  - Values into Action has been asked and agreed to work with self-advocacy groups to achieve this.

The money set aside to date will only go some way to the fulfilment of the Government's long-term aim.

A second challenge concerns tensions between different groups. Some follow the principles of Wolfensberger and believe in complete independence and insist that advocates should receive no rewards in terms of remuneration and academic credits. Others are more pragmatic, perhaps paying some advocates or operating within charitable organisations providing a contracted-out service.

These tensions are likely to continue to exist, but it will be important to ensure that the vision of the advocacy movement is not lost.

Conclusion   When Barb Goode addressed the General Assembly of the
United Nations in 1992, she said:

*'Our voice may be a new one to many of you but you should better
get used to hearing it.*

Many of us still have to learn how to speak up.

*Many of you still have to learn how to listen to us and how to
understand us.*

*We demand that you give us the right to make choices and decisions
regarding our own lives.*

*We are tired of people telling us what to do, what they want.
Instead, let us work together as a team.'*

That is the ongoing task.

> **Further reading**
>
> Brooke, J. & Harris, J. (2000) *Pathways to Citizen
> Advocacy.* Kidderminster: British Institute of Learning
> Disabilities.
>
> Foundation for People with Learning Disabilities
> (2000) *Everyday Lives, Everyday Choices for People with
> Learning Disabilities and High Support Needs.* London:
> FPLD.
>
> Foundation for People with Learning Disabilities
> (2000) *Choice Discovered.* A video and training
> materials. London: FPLD.
>
> Mental Health Foundation (1996) *Building
> Expectations: Opportunities and services for people with a
> learning disability.* London: MHF.

References

Department of Health (2001) *Valuing People: A new strategy for learning disability for the 21st century.* London: The Stationery Office.

Emerson, E., Hatton, C., Felce, D. & Murphy, G. (2000) *Learning Disabilities: The Fundamental Facts.* London: Mental Health Foundation.

Goode, B. (1992) Address to the UN General Assembly. *ILSMH News* **14** Brussels, ILSMH (now Inclusion International). Quoted in: L. Ward (Ed) (1998) *Innovations in Advocacy and Empowerment.* Chorley: Lisieux Hall Publications.

O'Brien, J. & Tyne, A. (1981) *The Principle of Normalisation: A foundation for effective services.* London: Campaign for Mentally Handicapped People (Community and Mental Handicap Educational and Research Association).

Wolfensberger, W. (1983) *Reflections on the Status of Citizen Advocacy.* Toronto: National Institute of Mental Retardation.

 Part Three

KEY AREAS

WRITTEN BY
Michelle McCarthy

Chapter 11

INTIMATE LIVES

*Sexuality and people
with learning disabilities*

In the past, the sexual rights, needs and feelings of people with learning disabilities were ignored or deliberately repressed. But more recently (ie since the 1970s), the sexuality of people with learning disabilities has been acknowledged. Most services today recognise their role in helping adults with learning disabilities express their sexuality. However, this is a difficult and delicate task, as sexual matters are not usually freely discussed in our society. Sexual matters are generally considered to be highly personal to the individual. Consequently, addressing sexuality issues can give rise to feelings of embarrassment, fear or shame on the part of both staff and service users.

Defining term Table 1 overleaf lists some terms you should be familiar with. Note that they are not always used in exactly the same way by everybody, but the definitions given here will provide you with a good starting point for further reading and discussion.

	Table 1	Definitions of terms

Term	Definition
Sex	the biology of a person, whether they are female or male. Therefore a sex difference would be that women give birth to children
Gender	a culturally shaped group of attributes and behaviours assigned to the male or female. Therefore, a gender difference would be that women (rather than men) usually look after children
Sexuality	the organisation, expression and direction of sexual desire, love, loyalty, passion, affection, intimacy
Sexual identity	a sense of one's own sexuality
Sexual orientation	a natural inclination towards a particular sexual identity
Homophobia	an irrational fear or disgust of lesbians and gay men
Heterosexism	a belief that heterosexuality is more normal, more natural, more morally right than homosexuality

Acknowledge people's aspirations

Many, though by no means all, people with learning disabilities wish to form intimate adult relationships. These are often expressed in terms of wanting a girl/boyfriend, wanting to be engaged or married, wanting to have children. How far these are the actual desires of individuals and how far it is people wanting to conform to society's norms and expectations is as impossible to separate out for people with learning disabilities, as it is for other people. Nevertheless, what we can observe is:

- people's stated desires do not always match their actual behaviour (eg a man with learning disabilities may say he wants a girlfriend and wants to get married, yet only seeks out other men for sexual partners)

- the aspirations or priorities of families and service providers often do not match what people with learning disabilities want (eg families and services often see the risks in sexual relationships, whereas people with learning disabilities tend to see the benefits).

 Box 1: A framework for understanding and responding to sexuality issues

- Acknowledge people's aspirations

- Respect people's rights

- Help people understand risks

- Help people understand their responsibilities

The harsh reality of life for many people with learning disabilities is that their aspirations may be not be met, ie they may not achieve a happy and lasting relationship. It is important to remember that many other people do not achieve this either.

For example, in many societies there is a very high divorce rate and countless other people, regardless of their sexual orientation, do not manage to sustain the kinds of sexual relationships they would ideally like. In a sense, that is just the way life is and little can be done about it. But, importantly, many barriers are unnecessarily put in the way of people with learning disabilities and there is much that can and should be done about that.

Respect people's rights

Since sexuality issues have started to be addressed, there has been constant debate about the sexual rights of people with learning disabilities. Most staff in learning disability services tend to say, when asked, that people with learning disabilities should have the same sexual rights as everybody else. This is as it should be (except there are some important legal differences regarding being able to consent to sex; see page 159), but does not get us very far in determining what those rights might be. The suggested list of rights in **Box 2**, opposite, would, I think, be accepted by most people.

Box 2: A list of sexuality rights

- to be acknowledged as a sexual being and therefore allowed any sexual expression within the law

- to have privacy for sexual expression

- to have access to appropriate sex education and support

- to have access to the means of protection from unwanted pregnancy, sexually transmitted infections, sexual assault

- to be recognised as a man or woman (not a genderless person)

- to have children?

The last in the list has a question mark against it to reflect the fact that this right is not widely accepted, but in fact still highly contested for people with learning disabilities.

Help people understand risks

There are certain inherent risks to engaging in sexual behaviours and these are essentially the same for people with learning disabilities as for anyone else. **Broadly speaking, there are three types of risks:**

1 **Physical** (eg pregnancy, sexually transmitted infections, damage to sensitive parts of the body)

2 **Emotional or psychological** (eg being upset or rejected by a partner, being abused)

3 **Social** (eg gaining a 'bad' reputation, paying the price for disregarding social norms).

It is not the role of staff in learning disability services to help service users avoid all risks. This is not possible. However, it is appropriate to do the following:

- help people with learning disabilities understand **what risks** they may face

- help them judge which are **worthwhile risks** (eg understanding there are no guarantees of success at the start of a new relationship)

- help them learn what **steps to take to avoid serious and unpleasant consequences** (eg of sexual abuse, unwanted pregnancy, HIV/Aids).

Help people understand their responsibilities

Learning disability services have responsibilities to their users, for example, to provide proactive sex education and support, and to provide an environment which is conducive to a responsible and adult attitude to sex (by ensuring privacy and respect). However, people with learning disabilities also have responsibilities when it comes to sexuality. At a minimum level these would include:

- trying to understand the potential consequences of their behaviour

- to ask for help with things they don't understand

- not to abuse or offend others

- to accept and take on board the information and support offered.

Clearly, being able to take responsibility in the above ways will be closely related to the level of learning disability a person has and their capacity to understand and act on their responsibilities.

Sexual health

A broad definition of sexual health would be '*sexual activity which enables a person to keep physically and psychologically well*'. However, in the learning disability field, a much narrower range of concerns have predominated and these have concerned the avoidance of sexually transmitted infections, most notably, HIV (Human Immuno-deficiency Virus). Although people with learning disabilities as a 'group' would not appear in any list of those most at risk of HIV, nevertheless if they engage in high risk sexual activities, they (like anyone else) clearly can become infected themselves and pass the infection on to others.

Therefore, in recent years, efforts have been made in some learning disability services to:

- educate service users about safer sex

- educate staff about how they might assess and manage HIV risks (see **Chapter 5**).

As with the general population, those people with learning disabilities who are most at risk of HIV infection are those who have unprotected sex with multiple partners. This is particularly the case for men with learning disabilities who have sex with other men, outside of service settings eg in public toilets or similar venues (this is known as 'cottaging'). These men tend to be those with relatively mild and moderate learning disabilities, who go out and about independently and who thus have the opportunity to meet sexual partners in the above ways. Although all sexually active people with learning disabilities need to be given information, education and support around safer sexual behaviour, people with particularly high risk behaviours should be prioritised.

All safer sex education with people with learning disabilities must take into account the reality of their sexual lives. The fact is that there often are power imbalances in sexual relationships or in casual sexual encounters. This may be based on gender (ie men controlling the sexual activity and women not having much of a say about what happens) or it may be based on intellectual ability (eg if a man with learning disabilities is having sex with a non-disabled man). Such power imbalances usually make it very difficult indeed for people with learning disabilities to assert themselves. This means that any safer sex education must respond to this and try to help people in the difficult situations they find themselves in, not just simplistically advise always to use a condom.

Sexual abuse

Sexual abuse and exploitation of people with learning disabilities is unfortunately a very common occurrence. A lot of research and practice-based evidence has emerged in recent years which can leave us in no doubt about this. People with learning disabilities are vulnerable to sexual abuse for many reasons, including:

- being accustomed to being told what to do by others
- lack of education about sex and about abuse
- lack of self-esteem and assertiveness (ie not realising they have the right not to be abused)
- not being believed when they speak about what has happened
- living in environments where they are exposed to many potential perpetrators (other people with learning disabilities, staff, volunteers, etc)
- not being valued and protected members of society.

Consent

Only those people who have severe or profound learning disabilities are legally defined as being unable to consent to sexual relationships. For the majority – ie those with mild and moderate learning disabilities – the law applies to them in the same ways as it does for any other person. However, there can still be problems with determining consent to sex for some people. Consent to sex should only be seen as valid if the person genuinely understands what they are saying yes to and if they have a real option (ie no adverse consequences) of saying no. This means in practice that people need to understand the nature and the consequences of sexual acts, plus not experience any pressure, threats or fear in making their decision. The laws on sexual offences involving people with learning disabilities are currently changing, but will still follow the broad framework outlined above.

Sexuality in the context of race, culture and religion

In recent years there has been a growing recognition of the need to respect the diversity in race, culture and religion of people with learning disabilities. Many learning disability services now try to provide support which is sensitive to the specific needs of service users from minority ethnic backgrounds. Obviously, providing sexuality support should be no different. However, this is hard to do, as there are tensions and disagreements within and between cultures about various forms of sexual expression.

The kinds of tensions which might arise between people with learning disabilities, their families and services could include the following examples…

■ The parents of a Muslim woman with learning disabilities refuse permission for their daughter to attend a mixed personal relationships course.

- The family of a Roman Catholic man with learning disabilities does not want him to be taught about safer sex, as use of condoms is not sanctioned by their religion.

- The parents of an Asian woman with learning disabilities are arranging her marriage, but staff at her day service feel she does not understand what this means.

- A man with learning disabilities from an Orthodox Jewish background is known to have sex with other men, and believes his religion permits this, when in fact it does not.

Staff in learning disability services should take great care before making assumptions about what a particular culture's beliefs and practices about sexuality are. Where possible this should be discussed with the person with learning disabilities themselves. Where this is not possible, or to supplement that information, good practice would be to seek advice from a number of representatives of a culture, and, if appropriate, from the family.

To avoid potential conflict between individuals, their families and services, it is useful to recognise that all parties have a shared commitment to the wellbeing of the person with learning disabilities. Since, in practice, most sexuality work with people with learning disabilities prioritises safety issues, this provides a good basis for interventions which should satisfy all concerned. Perceived or real cultural influences should not be accepted as a reason to deny people with learning disabilities the information and skills they need to protect themselves from exploitation and abuse.

Conclusion People with learning disabilities have a right to support with the sexual side of their lives. Those supporting them need to be aware of the reality of people's lives and circumstances and tailor their support accordingly. Those who support them should also remember that although intimate relationships and sexual expression may be problematic for some people with learning disabilities, so they are for many other people too. This is easy to forget when it is always 'their' sexual lives under scrutiny, and not 'ours'.

Further reading

Craft, A. (1994) *Practice Issues in Sexuality and Learning Disabilities*. London: Routledge.

McCarthy, M. (1999) *Sexuality and Women with Learning Disabilities*. London: Jessica Kingsley.

Malhotra, S. & Mellan, B. (1996) Cultural and race issues in sexuality work with people with learning difficulties. *Tizard Learning Disability Review* **1** (4) 7–12.

Thompson, D. (1994) Sexual experience and sexual identity for men with learning disabilities who have sex with men. *Changes* **12** (4) 254–263.

WRITTEN BY
Margaret Flynn,
Sheila Hollins and
Wendy Perez

Chapter 12

BEING SEEN...
TO BE HEALTHY!

*Accessing healthcare,
supporting healthy
lifestyles*

Introduction

People with learning disabilities are not as healthy as they should be.
People would be healthier if they had things to do in the day.
Unemployment and being in day centres are not good for your health.
Communication matters if people need health care. Consent is a
problem. We need things to be explained when we go to see a doctor so
that we know what is going to happen. We have to use the same NHS
services as everyone else. The NHS is for all of us. Community Learning
Disability Teams only offer a 9–5 service so it is not right to keep referring
us there. We are all learning from the work we are doing at St George's
Hospital: us, the Community Learning Disability Teams and the students.
I work as a training advisor and I teach medical students and nurses.
The students have more time for people. We all need help when we're
not well, and help to stay well. Some staff think families are interfering
when they help with health, but if they don't help in hospitals, people
have a bad time. I'm assertive, but some people aren't and that's why
there should be people to help. I'm interested in accessible information
and that's why I work on the Books Beyond Words Series. We've done
a lot of work on health for this.

Wendy Perez

What are the problems? As Wendy Perez's introduction illustrates, good health or its absence is the result of lots of connected factors. There is growing evidence that people with learning disabilities do not access GPs and general hospital services as much as they could and should. **Research has shown that people with learning disabilities experience a greater variety, number and frequency of health problems than the rest of the population, particularly those:**

- who do not move without help
- who need different kinds of assistance with feeding, including tube feeding
- with epilepsy
- who are incontinent
- who have diagnosed conditions, such as Down's syndrome

...and yet they use the NHS much less than they need to.

As a result, many people with learning disabilities have undetected health problems that cause unnecessary suffering and which limit the quality and/or length of their lives. There is evidence that learning disabilities may occur more frequently amongst some ethnic groups, and yet they receive less help from all services, including health services.

Overall, very few people with learning disabilities access health-screening services or benefit from health promotion activities. Knowledge of family health histories (including painful encounters with NHS personnel), family beliefs and practices, their own histories of contact with health professionals and the ways they see and respond to illness may be unknown and/or not sought. Their understanding of their bodies, of essential health routines, of sexual health and safe sex, of healthy diets and lifestyles, and even their medication, varies enormously.

Lying behind these disadvantages are some powerful institutions, customs and practices:

- Some learning disability services have sought to provide comprehensive health services on their own eg in 'hospitals' that are not really hospitals and which fail to attend to people's life-long health needs.

- The wider NHS has failed to consider the needs of people with learning disabilities, relying on such specialist learning disability services as Community Teams, leaving the wider NHS unskilled in making their services accessible, acceptable and responsive.

- The NHS requires each of us to be proactive in maintaining and promoting our health, in responding to invitations offering appointments and in ensuring that we get regular, daily exercise, for example. If we do not read or communicate so easily, then health professionals rely on relatives and care-givers to help us.

Some starting points

There is no magic formula for making sure that the NHS is inclusive and more responsive. But there is no doubt that if ideas about improving the health of people with learning disabilities are to have a wide impact, we need to work with others, especially professionals in primary care and general hospital services. In this section, we suggest some 'starting points', based on our knowledge and experience of how some people with learning disabilities, their relatives, health and social care professionals are focusing their efforts.

1 **Becoming persistent and creative advocates for improved health and health care**

We are not born with the capacity for collective action, but in the process of becoming committed to the people and communities we know, live and work in, we learn that, with others, we can challenge what needs to be challenged and change things.

 Maureen accompanied **Jo**, a woman with learning disabilities who has arthritis, to see her GP. Maureen was dismayed that the GP declined to refer Jo to the local hospital's Rheumatology Department for better pain control. Maureen persisted and in the process (six visits later) learned about the importance of ensuring that people who are accompanied to see their GP are always supported by knowledgeable people. Maureen 'modelled' respectful ways of communicating with Jo, interpreting what the GP was saying to her in easy language. Jo's GP came to acknowledge that the astonishing changes in Jo's behaviour, movement and demeanour, arose from improved pain control. The actions of Maureen and the GP teach us all about loyalties, conflict and the respectful recognition of each other's knowledge.

2   **Learning with and from people with learning disabilities and their relatives about their family health histories and their experiences of health services**

Many parents freely recall the time that they learned that their child had a learning disability. If this was done with compassion, in ways that allowed them to make sense of what it meant, they are likely to have begun their relationship with the NHS with their child on the right footing. If the disclosure was less than sensitive, this may have resulted in wariness in their dealings with the NHS. Positive relationships, built on trust, are critical to ensuring that people with learning disabilities are assisted to access services that are available to everyone.

 When Shama made the time to find out from **Tricia**'s sisters about the health and illnesses of Tricia's relatives, she learned that her two sisters and an aunt had received treatment for breast cancer. Shama contacted Tricia's GP and, with support from the Practice Nurse and Tricia's sisters, over a period of three months, Tricia was prepared for mammography.

3   **Finding out about people's health education and health promotion experiences in their homes, at school, in colleges, day and residential services**

Health education is concerned with the communication of information about health. Health promotion involves empowerment, a process that enables us to assert our own health agendas and priorities. Health education and promotion materials tend to assume that people can read. Although there is a growing range of accessible resources (see page 174), their availability and importance is not widely known.

The National Curriculum does address health education, but it appears that insufficient efforts are made to link this with learning opportunities into adulthood.

 Wendy Perez assisted in the design and testing of *Looking After Yourself 'Down Below'*. She asked women in her women's group if they had had smear tests. Although they are in their 30s and 40s, none of them had been invited for a smear test. Within a month, having learned from Wendy of the importance of smear tests, they had smear tests.

 Tom encouraged residents in the residential service in which he worked to watch and talk about such TV soaps as 'ER', 'Casualty' and 'Peak Practice.' When one resident was preparing to go into hospital for an operation, their preparation with the Community Learning Disability Team nurse included recalling some of the episodes from these programmes.

4   Being attentive to, and acting on, changes to people's bodies

People whose communication is difficult to understand and/or who are dependent on others for their intimate care, have to rely on others to respond to their help-seeking behaviour. This might include tearful distress and self-injurious behaviour, for example. They also rely on others to notice and act on observable changes to their bodies.

As Bill and Mike assisted **Ian** in the bath, they noticed that Ian winced as his genitals were washed. Further, Ian made protective gestures as they proceeded to dry him. As this had not happened before, they talked to the home manager that evening, confirmed the necessity of arranging an appointment to see his GP the following day, and made a note in Ian's files. A testicular examination by the GP and subsequent tests confirmed that Ian had testicular cancer. As Ian's observed discomfort was acted upon immediately, he was offered necessary and effective treatment.

Another consequence of having limited communication is an inability to explain clearly about traumatic experiences and their impacts.

 Charlie was badly hurt in a mugging in his neighbourhood. After his physical injuries had been attended to, Charlie was irritable with his house mates and anxious about leaving the house. Mary understood the importance of getting the police to take the assault seriously. Eventually, the men who assaulted Charlie were caught and prosecuted and Mary supported Charlie in going to court and giving evidence. Gradually, Charlie has regained his confidence, although he continues to need support in walking around his neighbourhood.

5   Establishing and/or maintaining essential health routines

Most of us have acquired some understanding of health routines from our families and our peers. We respond to invitations for screening, make appointments to have our sight and hearing tested if we experience difficulties, take ourselves to a dentist every six months, and if we take medication, we notice that this gets reviewed. That some people do not appear to have health routines or have families who do not appear to value such routines, does not mean that they are in good health. Routines have to be established, maintained and valued for everybody.

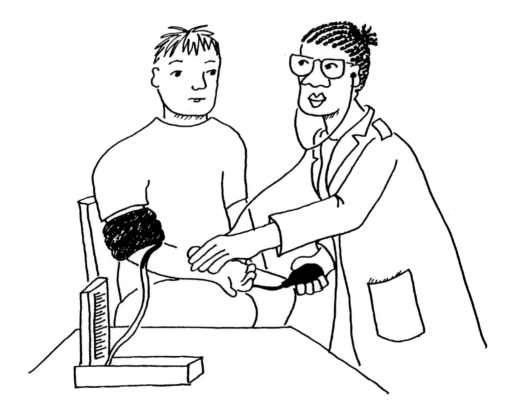

Jane's own experience of having a sister with Down's syndrome led her to ask about screening for thyroid disease for people with Down's syndrome in the day service in which she worked. With the support of the Community Learning Disability Team nurse, she contacted people's families and residential services and asked when people had last been screened and if they wanted support to access screening.

This initiative led to support staff making links with their own health experiences. Together, they considered these alongside the health care experiences of people they knew well, and matched them with those of the people they supported. This led them to ask such critical questions as *'Why are the women being excluded from screening?' 'How can we support the people we work with to get better and regular dental care?'* It was the beginning of profoundly important learning that was shared with new staff as they joined the service, to the benefit of everyone with learning disabilities.

6 Prioritising the support of people with learning disabilities in general hospitals

General hospitals may struggle to support their patients with learning disabilities. Families of and services for people with learning disabilities *both* express concern about hospital skills level and experience.

 Frank's sisters stayed with him as often as they could to ensure that he understood how to order his meals, and to make sure that he understood what procedures he should expect. They made sure they were present at clinical meetings, asking questions and explaining answers to Frank. Some staff began to communicate with Frank in ways that they learned he could follow. Frank's sisters prepared notes for the ward and clinical staff about Frank, about ways of getting the best from him, encouraging him to co-operate with post-operative treatment and the importance of using easy language with him. They also declined to sign Frank's Consent to Treatment form, explaining that as he was over 18, understood the risks and benefits of the operation and was competent to sign for himself, he should do so (see **Resources**, p174).

7 Exploring how your service might become more 'health conscious' and taking steps to change

For many people, leaving school involves the loss of opportunities for sport, exercise and the fun of active group activities. It has been observed that the sedentary lives of many adults with learning disabilities resemble those of many older people.

Megan's interest in cooking led to revising the menus and, in turn, the diets of everybody in the unit. Over time, and in consultation with a dietician, more interesting and nutritious diets led to a key change in people's health, with few requiring further medication for constipation.

Vernon was shocked to see that since **Tariq** had been in the residential service in which he worked, he had put on four stones in weight in less than four years. As his new keyworker, he hoped that Tariq would share some of his own interests, including weight training. Talking to Tariq's mother and brother, he learned that Tariq had enjoyed sports at school and that he had been a keen runner. Vernon also learned of their distress that Tariq's physique had changed totally. A visit to the practice nurse of the Primary Health Care Team to establish that he was well enough to commence graduated exercise was instrumental in changing Tariq's life. Now, Tariq and Vernon do weight and circuit training every week. They also initiated a brisk, daily walk in the park after the evening meal. Tariq is more engaged with his surroundings, happier and a lot fitter.

Having a learning disability does not mean that poor health and unresponsive health care are inevitable. The task of making changes is a long distance event that begins with such small steps as those we have described. Creative advocates learn with and from people with learning disabilities and their families. They gather tried and tested ideas, such as those described, to make changes and teach others what they have learned in the process. What we do is important, particularly if we are working in unsympathetic settings or systems. When the influence of these settings and systems wanes, whether they are followed by more responsive or negligent practices, depends on all of us.

Concluding thoughts

We want to go to see the doctor and to go for hospital appointments like everyone else and to have the time we need. This year, someone who wasn't my regular consultant said, *'People like you are just seeking attention'*. My regular consultant is still investigating this because he doesn't agree. It is because of things like this that I have got interested in health. I think that if we do better for people with learning disabilities, what we have done will be good for other people too. I want better treatment and I had to be assertive because the other doctor was so rude. You can be assertive when you know things. Everyone finds difficult things easier to understand in pictures. Books Beyond Words help people who can read and people who can't.

I want to change people's views and ideas about my health and other people's health. I'm a creative advocate and I want to be more of a creative advocate on other people's behalf. When I say I want to brush up my advocacy skills, they say, *'You're dangerous enough as you are!'*. I want to see more dangerous and creative advocates – that's why I work in a medical school.

Wendy Perez

Resources

Hollins, S., Bernal, J. & Gregory, M. (1996) *Going to the Doctor.* Books Beyond Words Series. London: Gaskell/St George's Hospital Medical School and the Royal College of Psychiatrists.

> *This shows in pictures what may happen when a man and woman go to the doctor. It is intended to help prepare adults with learning disabilities for a visit to their GP. As with all of the Books Beyond Words Series, it includes a guide for people who may accompany men and women with learning disabilities when they visit their primary health care team – as well as information for the primary health care team.*

> It is available from the Royal College of Psychiatrists, 17 Belgrave Square, London SW1X 8PG. Tel. 020 7235 2351. It costs £10.00, including postage and packing.

Hollins, S., Avis, A. & Cheverton, S. (1998) *Going into Hospital.* Books Beyond Words Series. London: Gaskell/St George's Hospital Medical School and the Royal College of Psychiatrists.

> *This book is designed to support a man going into hospital to have a planned operation and a woman going into hospital having been admitted as an emergency. As with all the Books Beyond Words Series, it is suggested that the pictures most relevant to the people requiring support are selected for discussion.*

> It is available from the Royal College of Psychiatrists, 17 Belgrave Square, London SW1X 8PG. Tel. 020 7235 2351. It costs £10.00, including postage and packing.

Department of Health (1998) *The Healthy Way: How to stay healthy – A guide for people with learning disabilities.* Wetherby: Department of Health.

> *This was designed with people with learning disabilities and, using cartoons and easy-to-understand language, it describes their experiences, ideas and concerns about accessing health care as a series of discussion points. The guide is accompanied by (i)*

an audio cassette, using the voices of a man and woman with learning disabilities, and (ii) a board game designed by self-advocates in Sefton.

It is FREE and available from the Department of Health, PO Box 410, Wetherby, LS23 7LN.

Joseph Rowntree Foundation (1999) *Findings 029: Adults with learning difficulties' involvement in health care decision-making.* York: JRF.

This is a summary of research by Kirsty Keywood, Sara Fovargue and Margaret Flynn. The full report, Best Practice? Health Care Decision-Making By, With and For Adults with Learning Disabilities, *deals with the law about adults with learning disabilities making decisions about their health and it includes ideas about adjusting the ways in which support is offered to positively impact on people's decision-making.*

The full report is available from the National Development Team, Albion Chambers, Albion Wharf, Albion Street, Manchester M1 5LN for £5.50, including postage and packing. The National Development Team can be contacted by phone. Tel. 0161 228 7055.

The Findings summaries are free and available from the Joseph Rowntree Foundation, The Homestead, 40 Water End, York, YO30 6WP. Tel. 01904 629241.

An accessible version of the Findings, *Plain Facts: Making decisions about health care*, Issue 15, which includes an audio cassette, was published in 2000. It is available from the Norah Fry Research Centre, 3 Priory Road, Bristol, BS8 1TX. Tel. 0117 923 8137.

Hollins, S. & Perez, W. (2000) *Looking After My Breasts* and Hollins, S. & Downer, J. (2000) *Keeping Healthy 'Down Below'.* Books Beyond Words Series. London: Gaskell/St George's Hospital Medical School and the Royal College of Psychiatrists.

These books were designed to make communication about women's health screening easier. They describe in sequence the events of receiving an invitation letter for screening, deciding whether to attend, preparing for a screening appointment, attending, getting the results and being recalled for further tests. As with all the Books Beyond Words Series, this has been 'tried out' with groups of people with learning disabilities, and for these books, women.

The books accompany a publication of the National Screening Committee (2000) *Good Practice in Breast and Cervical Screening for Women with Learning Disabilities* and two leaflets, *50 or over? Breast screening is for you* and *Having a smear test.*

These are FREE and available from the NHS Cancer Screening Programmes, The Manor House, 260 Ecclesall Road South, Sheffield S11 9PS. Their telephone number is 0114 271 1060.

Hollins, S. & Horrocks, C. (2002) *Mugged* describes a man's experiences of being mugged and the ways in which he is supported to feel safe again.

All of these books are available from the Royal College of Psychiatrists, 17 Belgrave Square, London SW1X 8PG. Tel. 020 7235 2351. They cost £10.00 each, including postage and packing.

WRITTEN BY
Steven Carnaby

Chapter 13

BEING WHO YOU ARE

KEY WORDS

labels

multiple learning
disability

profound learning
disability

stigmatise

sensory disabilities

terminology

Working with people with profound and multiple learning disabilities

'We still don't know how to work with them.'

'It's difficult to work with people when you're not getting any feedback.'

These quotes are from research participants interviewed as part of a research project reported by Phoebe Caldwell in her book, *Getting in Touch*. Such comments can be typical of those made by people supporting individuals with profound disabilities. For some there is frustration at not knowing what to do as a worker, what is expected. For others, there may be fear or even repulsion in finding oneself face to face with a person who they perceive to be so very different from themselves – perhaps physically as well as intellectually. These feelings need to be acknowledged, as they are likely to obstruct any effective work and more importantly, will stop the worker from getting to know the individual as a person with his or her unique personality, interests, likes and dislikes.

People with a profound learning disability (PLD) or profound and multiple learning disabilities (PMLD) form a small but significant section of the learning disabled population. It is increasingly recognised that people with PLD or PMLD need specific types of support that are likely to differ in nature and intensity from that needed by individuals with moderate or mild learning disabilities.

This chapter begins by defining profound, and profound and multiple, disability, and describes some of the key implications for service providers. A case study is used to illustrate ways in which multidisciplinary teams can work collaboratively with service users and their supporters. Emphasis is placed on principles of good practice aimed at minimising the social exclusion experienced by many people with high support needs.

Definitions: who are we talking about?
Before thinking about what support is needed by people with PLD or PMLD, it is important to be clear about the group of people we are talking about. Various labels and terms have been used, including:

- profound disabilities
- profound and multiple disabilities
- high support needs
- complex needs
- complex and multiple disabilities.

All of the above terms may be useful, but the language used must be agreed and used consistently within an organisation or service to avoid confusion. As a starting point for discussion that would take place within local services, some definitions are offered in **Box 1**, opposite.

Box 1: Definitions

As mentioned in **Chapter 1**, a 'significant impairment' is indicated by an IQ score of below 70 (the average for the general population is 100). **People with profound learning disabilities** are estimated as having an IQ in the 'below 20' range – although measurement at this level is not possible. People with profound learning disabilities are functioning at the very early stages of development, and have skills at a level that are acquired by 'typically' developing children in the first year of life.

People with profound and multiple learning disabilities experience disabilities *in addition to* their learning disabilities. These may include one or more of the following in any combination: sensory or physical disabilities, mental health problems, autism, challenging or self-injurious behaviour.

Being consistent with language also helps to ensure that the extent of an individual's disability is acknowledged and respected. While labels of any kind have the potential to stigmatise, sensitive use of clear terminology maps out what people need and indicates the types of support that are likely to be most appropriate. Unclear and inconsistent use of labelling can put people at risk of receiving inadequately planned support. This can compromise the individual's quality of life, and in some cases could lead to poor physical and/or psychological health.

Designing services While general definitions are possible, it is important to note that like any population, people with profound disabilities form a very diverse group. Support must be designed at a very individual, person-centred level, which is always about knowing people well. Designing effective support consists of thorough assessment of what the person needs, careful planning of support informed by the assessment, and a clear method of evaluating the support provided to determine its effectiveness.

In her book, *Person to Person* (1998), Phoebe Caldwell talks about how she begins this process, and its value:

'*...I want to know, as far as possible, how* [people with profound disabilities] *perceive their world – how it feels to them. Within the parameters of where they feel safe, how can we enlarge and enrich their experience? How can we increase their confidence and help them to "feel good" about themselves and others?*'

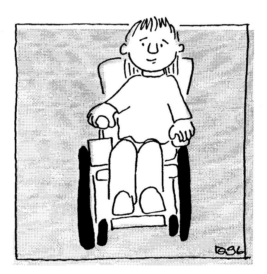

Assessment

For people with PLD or PMLD, the nature and complexities of their disabilities mean that a thorough multidisciplinary assessment is essential. Assessment needs to be across professions, with close collaboration and inclusion of the individual and his or her family or carers. A working list of principles is provided in **Box 2**, opposite.

Box 2: Principles of the assessment process

- Spend time with the person in a range of different settings (eg at home and at the day centre); watch how s/he responds to different people and different situations.

- Try to establish how the person shows like or dislike.

- Support and participate in the completion of standardised assessment tools used by professionals from the local community team. These tools are used to assess areas such as the individual's communication skills, their vision and hearing or their level of social functioning. Many of these require information from informants other than the service user – give careful thought to who the most appropriate informants might be.

- Consult with the individual's GP or the local community learning disability nurse and ask for a health assessment to be completed (eg the 'OK Health Check').

- Spend time getting to know the individual's family and/or significant others. Respect for the individual's personal history and social context is a key element of good practice.

- Observe the individual's personal relationships, and the extent to which they seem *meaningful to him or her.*

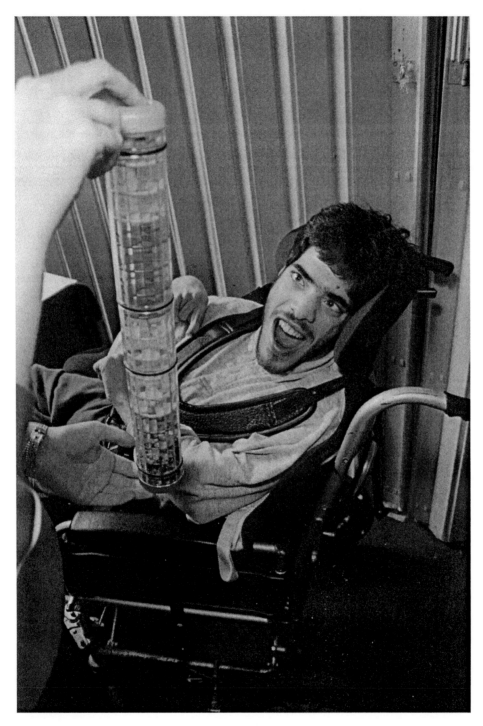

Photograph supplied by Mencap

Planning support

A thorough assessment will produce a wealth of information, and may well identify a number of areas that could be addressed. It may be more practical to identify the most pressing issues and address those, rather than try to meet all of the identified needs at once.

Planning is likely to take place within an individual planning process. The development of person-centred planning is now seen as good practice, where the individual is at the heart of the process and is involved as much as possible. Decision-making about the design of the person's support is likely to take place in a meeting, and this can easily exclude the person and sometimes any relatives attending. Some useful pointers for ensuring that meetings, and the rest of the planning process, remain person-centred are listed in **Box 3**, overleaf.

A useful planning process that is felt to be effective for people with profound disabilities is **Essential Lifestyle Planning**. This is a way of establishing what is 'essential' to the individual, and helps record how s/he communicates likes and dislikes. People in the group supporting the individual might ask themselves a number of key questions, and come to some consensus as to what might be true for the person. For example, it might be useful to ask:

- What would a 'good' day be like for this person?
- What would a 'bad' day be like?
- What do we think makes him/her happy?
- What do we think makes him/her sad?
- What do we need to know/do to support this person?

Box 3: Good practice in individual planning

If the person attends the planning meeting...

■ Consider whether attending part, or all, of the meeting will be meaningful for the person.

■ Avoid talking over his or her head – refer conversation back, maintain eye contact and use visual prompts or objects of reference to indicate what is being discussed.

■ Think carefully about who should attend. Has the individual met all of the participants before? If not, why are they there?

■ Consider the venue and time of day carefully. Is this a room where the individual feels comfortable? Is there optimal lighting if they have a visual impairment? Are they likely to make other associations with the function of the room (eg the room is used for dinner or physiotherapy)? Is the meeting straight after lunch when the individual might feel sleepy?

■ Make the individual's involvement the focal point of the meeting. Use photographs, video footage, scrapbooks, sensory and other objects to prompt discussion and encourage the individual to respond.

■ Consult with the local speech and language therapist to ensure that any appropriate communication aids are available to the person.

■ Make sure that the meeting remains focused and does not go on too long.

If the individual DOES NOT attend the meeting...

■ Ensure that the decision for the individual to not attend is discussed and agreed amongst a wider group of people involved. Record the process and ensure that the decision is reviewed when the next meeting is held.

■ Collect information with and about the person that can be shared at the meeting (eg video of being involved in favourite activities, holiday photographs etc).

■ Ensure that the meeting is positive – focus on strengths and areas for development, rather than a list of what the person 'cannot do' or problem behaviours.

Note

In practice, it is rare that the individual will not be able to make ANY contribution. Participation can take many forms. For example, using a projector to project images on to the wall of the person doing things s/he enjoys; playing tapes of 'favourite' sounds (eg leaves rustling or police sirens, or pieces of music). The individual's reactions to these different stimuli can be a powerful means of presenting aspects of his/her life to the meeting – in ways that s/he can influence and control.

Box 3: Good practice in individual planning
(cont.)

In both cases...

- Focus on strengths and interests as well as areas for development.

- Keep it positive – try to keep challenging behaviour and health-related issues to separate meetings unless they have direct relevance for the decision being made.

- Make sure that family members and/or advocates are given a central role in any decision-making.

Evaluating interventions

The ways we support people with profound disabilities, our interventions, need to be evaluated to check that they are achieving what was intended. This can be done in a number of ways, but will need to be tied directly to the nature of the support being provided. Examples of measures used to evaluate interventions include:

- **a rating scale** completed by staff to monitor an individual's reaction when offered a new activity

- **a graph**, to plot, for example, the frequency of head-banging before and after an intervention, that aims to engage the individual in alternative behaviours

- **a questionnaire** administered to family members seeking to establish their perception of an individual's reaction to a new short break service.

A developmental approach to support

Providing effective support for people with PLD or PMLD requires a collaborative approach that is developmentally appropriate for the individual concerned. Some find this approach difficult, as they feel that it compromises the individual's dignity and right to be respected as an adult.

However, the increasing evidence base, emerging to support the use of developmental approaches (see **Further reading**, p188), suggests that acknowledging an individual's level of functioning is essential if we are to support their development, enhance their engagement and encourage them to form meaningful relationships with other people. If handled sensitively, it can be argued that adopting a developmental approach is the clearest way of showing respect for an individual.

See **Case study**, opposite.

This approach to understanding Sofia's world has several themes...

- Assessment is concerned with Sofia's relationships and how she interacts with her world.
- Her developmental level and interests are placed at the centre of any planning of support.
- Everybody that knows Sofia well is involved and their perspectives valued.
- Interventions build on her interests and advocate one-to-one time and support as good practice.

Summary

People with PLD or PMLD can be at high risk of social exclusion, within services, as well as in the wider community. Services have a responsibility to work collaboratively across professional disciplines and with carers and families to plan effective support, both with and for individuals. Taking a

 **Case study: Sofia**

Sofia is 21 and lives with her parents. She has profound learning disabilities, uses a wheelchair and wears strong glasses. The community nurse working with Sofia noticed that she had started becoming very withdrawn, not maintaining eye contact and refusing to eat. Staff at Sofia's day centre had also noticed that she had stopped being as vocal and was engaging in self-involved behaviour (repeatedly playing with her fingers).

Sofia's community nurse decided to instigate a multidisciplinary assessment. This involved the speech and language therapist, the clinical psychologist, Sofia's parents, the occupational therapist and staff at Sofia's day centre. The process consisted of assessing:

- social functioning – conducted by the clinical psychologist in consultation with Sofia's parents
- Sofia's activity programme – conducted by the occupational therapist
- interview with the day centre staff
- observation of Sofia both at home and at the day centre.

Information from the assessments was collated and a planning meeting held. Sofia attended for part of the meeting – her keyworker from the day centre supported her to show video footage of Sofia taking part in activities, while her parents played audio tape of Sofia singing along to songs with her mother.

The meeting agreed that evidence from the assessment suggested that Sofia was functioning in the early stages of development and would need a significant amount of one-to-one time to make sense of her environment. It was also observed that such support was not readily available during the day, and Sofia was finding it difficult to participate in activities. She was often in groups of three people or more, most of whom were more assertive than her. This was possibly leading to feelings of being out of control and ultimately to depression, a possible explanation for her reluctance to eat.

A plan was drawn up which built in one-to-one sessions, providing Sofia with opportunities for developing relationships and engaging in meaningful activities. These activities were designed to build on Sofia's apparent interest in music (ie singing songs) and provide her with opportunities for interacting at her own pace.

Three months after the planning meeting, a review of the intervention was held. Video footage was shown of Sofia working with staff at the centre and community team members. Supporters encouraged Sofia to take part in turn-taking exchanges, singing her favourite songs and playing musical instruments. This work was *developmentally appropriate** in that it focused on Sofia's skills and encouraged her to interact at her pace and on her initiative. The video suggested that when Sofia was interacting in this way, she tended to not spend time playing with her fingers and was able to increase her eye contact with her interactive partner.

Note: based on the principles of *Intensive Interaction* – see **Further reading** on p188.

developmental approach within a thorough assessment process helps to ensure that any intervention is person-centred. Highly individualised support that is regularly evaluated can provide people with PLD or PMLD with a quality of life that consists of much more than just having physical needs met. Innovative and creative thinking can lead to people who were once seen as unable to communicate, and without the ability to learn, having the support to lead lives that are full of opportunities, choice, and meaningful relationships.

Further reading

Caldwell, P. (1996) *Getting in Touch*. Brighton: Pavilion.

Caldwell, P. (1998) *Person to Person*. Brighton: Pavilion.

Lacey, P. & Ouvray, C. (1998) *People with Profound and Multiple Learning Disabilities: A collaborative approach to meeting complex needs*. London: David Fulton.

Nind, M. & Hewett, D. (2001) *Intensive Interaction: A practice guide*. Kidderminster: BILD.

Ware, J. (1996) *Creating Responsive Environments for People with Profound and Multiple Learning Disabilities*. London: David Fulton.

WRITTEN BY
Peter Baker

Chapter 14

CONFRONTATION OR COMMUNICATION?

*Supporting people whose
behaviour challenges us*

What is 'challenging behaviour'?

Those involved in the care of people with learning disabilities are very likely to come across individuals who behave in ways that could be seen as challenging. Some researchers have suggested that approximately 10–15% of people with learning disabilities exhibit challenging behaviour. The term 'challenging behaviour' may seem rather vague in that it may cover a very wide range of behaviours. However, there is broad agreement that the term refers to **behaviours that have a negative impact on the person's quality of life or the quality of life of the people with whom they live**.

Two examples will serve to illustrate this range. The first is a man who will sing nursery rhymes at the top of his voice for hours at a time, the second, a man who will attack those around him, biting and scratching. Both behaviours, although very different, have a significant impact on those individuals and those who provide their care. The first person's behaviour would draw attention to the individual in public and irritate carers; the second would provoke fear and anxiety in carers, making them reluctant to come into contact with the person. Both of these people suffered in terms of their quality of life. The 'challenge' would be for carers to reduce the behaviour and, perhaps more importantly, make sure the person enjoyed a better quality of life.

Why do people exhibit challenging behaviour?

When working with people who present challenging behaviour it is inevitable that we will ask ourselves *why* the person does it. This is an extremely important question, as the conclusion will determine what we do to manage the behaviour. For an understanding to be useful, it should give us an indication of what we could do to reduce the behaviour, and also give us some idea of when the behaviour is likely to occur.

Often, the explanations for challenging behaviour given by carers will be things like frustration, anger, spite, greed, sadness, etc. These are all factors that lie within the person, ie *internal* factors. Whilst they may contain some grains of truth, they are not really useful in the sense described above. They do not give us any ideas about what should be done to prevent or reduce the behaviour; neither do they give us any indication as to when or under what circumstances the behaviour is likely to occur. The latter is important information, especially if the behaviour is aggression directed toward carers. If I might get hurt, I for one would want to know when the behaviour is likely to happen, in order that I could prepare. Therefore, it is generally considered more useful if *external* explanations are used that involve an understanding of what sort of situations trigger the behaviours.

For example: is the behaviour more likely to occur if: a request is made of the person?; they see something they want but can't get?; they are left with nothing to do?; or if they are not being given any attention?

Psychologists have developed the **Antecedent Behaviour Consequences (ABC)** approach to understanding challenging behaviour. This involves identifying the **antecedents** or triggers to the **behaviour** and also describing what happens as a result of the behaviour – the **consequences**.

 A typical scenario might be:

- **Antecedent** – asked to do the washing up
- **Behaviour** – self-injury and screaming
- **Consequences** – request withdrawn.

In this case, the reason the behaviour occurred was to escape from the demand. Thus the behaviour can be seen as **a form of communication** and the aim of understanding is to attempt to identify what the person is trying to say. Four main communication messages or reasons why people with learning disabilities present challenging behaviour have been identified:

- **demand avoidance**
- **tangible reinforcement**
- **self-stimulation**
- **attention.**

Demand avoidance would be similar to the above scenario, whereby the individual is rewarded by the removal of a demand.

Tangible reinforcement refers to situations where the individual would obtain objects or activities they like as a result of the behaviour.

Self-stimulation would be occasions where the behaviour itself is stimulating (and perhaps enjoyable) because it feels good.

Finally, the behaviour may be designed to communicate the need for **attention**.

Further consideration needs to be given to individual and environmental factors that make the types of communications referred to above more likely to occur (**Figure 1**).

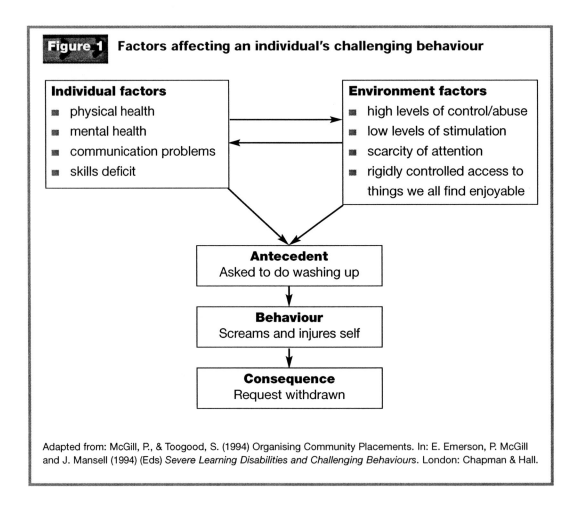

Figure 1 Factors affecting an individual's challenging behaviour

Individual factors
- physical health
- mental health
- communication problems
- skills deficit

Environment factors
- high levels of control/abuse
- low levels of stimulation
- scarcity of attention
- rigidly controlled access to things we all find enjoyable

Antecedent
Asked to do washing up

Behaviour
Screams and injures self

Consequence
Request withdrawn

Adapted from: McGill, P., & Toogood, S. (1994) Organising Community Placements. In: E. Emerson, P. McGill and J. Mansell (1994) (Eds) *Severe Learning Disabilities and Challenging Behaviours*. London: Chapman & Hall.

Individual factors

People with learning disabilities may well have specific needs that make them more vulnerable and hence more likely to present challenging behaviour. Some specific syndromes or conditions associated with learning disability have been shown to make challenging behaviour more likely. These would include factors such as epilepsy and mental health problems. However, there is a great deal of controversy surrounding this, and some authors have suggested that the relationship between these factors and challenging behaviour has been overemphasised. Less controversially, there are clearer links between communication, sensory and physical difficulties and the presentation of challenging behaviour.

Environment factors

When people are placed in environments that fail to meet the types of needs referred to above, it is almost inevitable that challenging behaviour will occur. Unfortunately, research suggests that often services are not well designed and will actively contribute to challenging behaviour. These may be characterised by:

- high levels of control and even abuse
- low levels of stimulation and a scarcity of attention
- rigidly controlled access to the things we all find enjoyable.

An individual with very few things in their life that they like may find themselves having their favourite thing removed, in an attempt to make them behave better. The person labelled 'attention-seeking' may be ignored, on the assumption that the attention is not needed or deserved.

This photograph was taken by Eugene Kariuki and was part of a lottery-funded project based in West London, run by ActionSpace.

Responding to challenging behaviour

Traditionally, the most common response to the management of challenging behaviour has been the **use of medication**. Very few people would argue that medication is the sole answer and some critics would suggest that the use of medication to manage behaviour, when there is no identified mental illness, is unethical. **Behavioural interventions** have long enjoyed the reputation of being effective in the management of challenging behaviour. **Modern behavioural approaches should:**

- consider the nature of the message communicated by the behaviour
- identify the relevant individual factors
- establish the nature of the individual's environment.

This emphasises the importance of **having a good understanding of the individual**.

Punishment

Most of us were raised with the overt use of punishment; when we were naughty we were reprimanded, had privileges withdrawn or were even smacked. It is perhaps understandable that care staff will use experiences of '**parenting-type management**' in their work with people with learning disabilities and challenging behaviour.

There are basic differences in the circumstances of normal child-rearing practices and care of people with learning disabilities that make the use of punishment **unacceptable**. Punishment has not worked thus far for these people, otherwise they would not have reached adulthood and still be presenting challenging behaviour – it is clearly **ineffective**. In addition, the rights of adults are very different from those of children and, in many cases, the use of punishment strategies may be potentially unlawful. Therefore, any intervention needs to take place within a framework that **respects the person's dignity and basic human rights**.

Interventions

The scope of the intervention should not be limited to bringing about a reduction in the behaviour. There should also be an expectation that the negative impact the challenging behaviour has on that individual's quality of life should be directly addressed. We should therefore be striving to bring about more **access, choice and control in the lives of people with learning disabilities**, whilst also encouraging the development of a **wider range of meaningful relationships**. Given these expectations and the likelihood that numerous factors will underlie the presentation of the challenging behaviour, interventions will necessarily involve many different elements which alone would be unlikely to be truly effective, but combined should bring about positive change.

Individual factors

The following factors may well be involved in the causation of the individual's challenging behaviour – they all lie within the individual and so the focus of the intervention would be to change that person in some way.

Physical health

If the person is in some degree of discomfort as a result of physical health difficulties, this distress may well be communicated by challenging behaviour, especially if they also have limited communication skills. Naturally, in such situations, it would be essential that the person receive the appropriate medical treatment in order to alleviate the discomfort.

Mental health

It is thought that people with learning disabilities are particularly prone to mental health difficulties. Challenging behaviour may well be exhibited as a result and appropriate psychiatric treatment should be offered. However, this is an area that is controversial and there is an argument that the high rates of mental health difficulties may be overstated. Often people are prescribed psychiatric medication simply to tranquillise them when there are no mental health problems. Clearly, such practices are unacceptable.

There is also growing evidence that people with learning disabilities who present challenging behaviour are extremely vulnerable to abuse and may well be traumatised by this. In this case, the individual should have access to psychological help and be provided with safe and supportive environments where they will hopefully learn that such things would not happen again.

Communication problems

Learning disability is often associated with communication problems (see **Chapter 6**). This may involve difficulty in expressing and in understanding. These difficulties are closely related to the presence of challenging behaviour, where the behaviour serves as some form of communication. In such situations, efforts designed to increase the individual's communication skills are likely, over time, to influence the occurrence of challenging behaviour.

Skill deficits

The nature of learning disability almost inevitably means the person will have some things they cannot do for themselves. As a result this will make them reliant upon carers to meet at least some of their needs or wants. This increases the chances of things going wrong for the person where, for example, nobody is available at the time the person requires, or the carer does not understand what the person wants or needs. This in turn may be associated with the occurrence of challenging behaviour. An obvious positive strategy here would be to teach that person the skills to do things for themselves, in order that they are less reliant upon those around them to meet their needs or wants.

Inevitably, in life there are occasions when we all experience things that are not quite to our liking. More often than not we cope because, although we might feel like having an outburst, we judge that this would actually make the situation worse for us. Some people with learning disabilities may not have acquired ways of coping with life's everyday irritations and may require coping skills to be taught in the same way as we teach independent living skills.

Environment factors

As stated above, if an environment does not meet the needs of the people who live there, those people are likely to protest and may well do this by exhibiting challenging behaviour. Clearly, any efforts designed to make the environment more supportive would be likely to bring about a reduction in challenging behaviour. These mismatches between need and environment will be very individual and require an understanding of the person and their situation as described above. Look at the table opposite for some suggestions of change in the person's environment that are related to the communication messages highlighted during the assessment process.

Communication message	Changes needed in the environment
Demand avoidance	If **demand avoidance** is a significant message communicated by the person's challenging behaviour, then perhaps serious consideration should be given to altering the amount or type of demands made upon the individual. The demands might be reduced in frequency, difficulty or duration, in order to make them more acceptable for the individual. In addition, strategies such as behavioural momentum, ie where the individual is approached and asked to perform tasks with which they are known to be highly likely to co-operate, thus establishing a momentum of co-operation before being asked to perform a more difficult task. Similarly, simply approaching the person and engaging in social 'chit-chat' before asking them to perform a task may well make co-operation more likely.
Tangible reinforcement	Where the message of the challenging behaviour is the need for an object or activity the person likes, ie **tangible reinforcement**, a straightforward change may be to make these things more freely available for the person in order that they might be able to 'help themselves'. If the person has physical or motor difficulties they may well require items in the environment to be specially adapted in order that they can use them independently. There would be some overlap between skills teaching here, whereby the person may also require some assistance in acquiring the skills to enable them to get things for themselves.
Self-stimulation	If the purpose for the behaviour is **self-stimulation** (ie doing something for the sensation felt at the time of doing it) it could be assumed that the environment lacks the right type or amount of stimulation for that person. Often people with learning disabilities who have also been labelled 'autistic' have unusual sensory needs or preferences and it would be unlikely that these needs would be met without specific planning.
Attention	Where the person is exhibiting challenging behaviour in order to get **attention**, perhaps the provision of more attention that was not dependent on challenging behaviour might assist in its reduction.

Changes could be introduced that are not related to any of the communication messages above. For example, if it were possible, removing the specific trigger for the behaviour would have an immediate effect on the occurrence of that behaviour. In addition, a theoretically endless list of changes could be introduced in that person's environment that would bring about a reduction in challenging behaviour, ranging from turning down the volume of the television to arranging for the person to move house.

Managing the occurrence of challenging behaviour

All the strategies above are designed to prevent the behaviour from occurring and, if based upon a good understanding of the person and properly implemented, should bring about gradual reduction, over time, in the challenging behaviour. However, there will still need to be plans in place that tell carers what they should do when the behaviour occurs.

Current thinking regarding the management of challenging behaviour states that the **positive prevention strategies** outlined above are essential, and that when planning what to do in response to the behaviour we should be focusing primarily on safety and not be overly concerned with what seems to be rewarding behaviour. This is sometimes difficult for carers to grasp, as it appears to conflict with 'parenting type management'. However, what is being proposed is that it is the positive prevention strategies that will make the difference in the long term. If we are in a situation where there are safety issues, then perhaps 'giving in', for example, is a good idea if it keeps everybody safe.

A good management plan should contain things that carers can do earlier in a difficult situation to 'nip it in the bud'. These are situations where you have some idea that difficult behaviour might occur. Perhaps you have noticed something in the environment that will typically trigger the behaviour, or the individual is starting to behave in a way that indicates that more serious behaviour is coming. These plans would again be individual and based upon strategies that have proven to work for that person and would include things like **distraction** and **calming** techniques.

Physical interventions

It is generally recognised that there will be rare occasions that may require carers to physically intervene with the client to prevent injury to the person or to others. In order to be within a sound legal and ethical framework the following principles should be followed...

- A risk assessment of situations where the management of challenging behaviour might involve physical intervention should be carried out in order that all other alternatives have been ruled out.

- Consideration should be given as to whether that individual is capable of consenting to the physical intervention. If so, their consent should be sought. If not, wide-ranging consultation should be conducted, including the individual's advocate, relatives, appropriately qualified and experienced professionals, etc.

- If the desired outcome for that individual is a reduction in the frequency, duration or impact of their challenging behaviour, an intervention plan should be devised with the appropriate balance between reactive strategies and prevention.

- An individualised **written** management plan should be constructed, including steps required to prevent the behaviour from either occurring at all or escalating.

- All care staff working with that individual should be trained as a team and be **competent** in the execution of this plan.

- All use of physical intervention should be **recorded**.

- The use of physical interventions should be **reviewed** to ensure that they are not being used to excess, they continue to promote the safety of service users and staff, and only those interventions detailed in the written management plan are being used.

Summary Understanding the communication, individual and environmental factors underlying an individual's challenging behaviour is a vital requirement for an effective intervention plan. This plan should not only hope to achieve reduction in challenging behaviour, but also achieve a better quality of life for that person. Given the range of influences on the person that leads to the challenging behaviour and the wide range of outcomes expected, interventions should:

- have many elements

- address individual and environmental factors

- consider ways of reacting to the behaviour that ensure safety and prevent the situation from becoming worse.

Further reading

Allen, D. (in press) *Behaviour Management in Intellectual Disabilities: Ethical responses to challenging behaviour.*

Baker, P. A., LaVigna, G. W. & Willis, T. J. (1998) Understanding and Responding to Challenging Behaviour: A multi-element approach. In: W. Fraser, D. Sines and M. Kerr (Eds) *Hallas's Caring for People with Learning Disabilities* (9th edition.) London: Butterworth Heinemann.

Emerson, E. (2001) *Challenging Behaviour: Analysis and intervention in people with intellectual disabilities* (2nd edition). Cambridge: Cambridge University Press.

Emerson, E., McGill, P. & Mansell, J. (1994) *Severe Learning Disabilities and Challenging Behaviours: Designing high quality services* pp232–259. London: Chapman & Hall.

WRITTEN BY
Geraldine Holt

Chapter 15

TAKING THE STRAIN

KEY WORDS

distress

mental health

mental illness

positive evaluation

predisposing
factors

wellbeing

*Mental health and people
with learning disabilities*

Health is a state of physical and emotional wellbeing. All of us
have times of illness, either physical or mental. When a person is
mentally ill, his or her mind does not function as it usually does.
That person's thoughts, emotions, beliefs or ability to reason
change and behaviour is 'out of character'.

People from different cultures believe and do different things.
When someone has a mental illness, his or her behaviour differs
from the usual pattern and may stand out as different to those of
other people from the same culture.

Factors underpinning mental ill health

Mental ill health is common. Each of us is vulnerable to particular stresses, because of our genetic make-up and life experiences. **Mental ill health is commoner in people with a learning disability**, probably as they are more likely to have a number of **predisposing factors**. These factors are listed in **Box 1**, below.

Box 1: Predisposing factors for mental ill health

Genetic
Some kinds of mental illness tend to run in families eg mood disorders, such as depression; and some genetic conditions are associated with an increased risk of particular mental health problems eg people with Down's syndrome are at increased risk of developing Alzheimer's dementia.

Adverse environmental conditions, such as social isolation and bullying.

Sensory impairments (eg hearing difficulties) and communication difficulties

Physical ill health
Physical ill health itself can increase the risk of developing mental illness, as can certain medications, including some given to treat epilepsy.

Brain damage

Note: These risk factors can affect us all, but are more common in those with a learning disability.

Some of these risk factors can be reduced. For example, we might try to promote positive mental health by improving people's self-esteem in the way we treat them, teaching them ways to cope with stress (eg relaxation) or by increasing their ability to communicate (eg by using non-verbal means).

Case study

Two nursing colleagues facilitated a mental health promotion group ran as a series of workshops. The group was evaluated positively by those attending. It helped service users to recognise when they are stressed and to develop coping strategies for stress. They became more aware of mental ill health, especially depression and anxiety. The workshops also provided service users with information regarding the range of services available in their borough, not only clinical services, but also leisure, advocacy and support services.

Issues in assessment and diagnosis

It is often difficult to put feelings into words. People with autism find this especially hard, as do others with limited communication skills. People with mental illness may not be able to describe or understand what is happening to them. We need to be alert to a change in a person's demeanour and behaviour. Such changes may be due to ill health, either mental or physical, and need treatment. People with a learning disability may need support to access help. A GP may be able to offer advice and treatment themselves, put the person in contact with a self-help group or make a referral to a specialist service, such as to a counsellor, psychologist or psychiatrist.

Clearly, an individual's behaviour can change for lots of reasons not to do with ill health. People with a mental health problem are often feared or disliked because of the negative emotions that the label 'mental illness' produces. This is prejudice. We can all become mentally ill and it is very common. A person with a learning disability has often suffered prejudice, so that becoming mentally ill can be seen as another damaging label. We need to support the person with a learning disability appropriately, and this requires an open mind. The possibility of mental ill health should be considered as one of a number of reasons why a person seems to be 'not himself'. If I seem a bit low and off my food it may be that I've gone on a diet and I am missing my food! It may also be because I don't like what I'm being offered, or that I have a bug or am depressed. There are many possibilities. **Only by looking at the whole picture can we start to understand what is going on.**

Case study: Susan

Even quite unusual behaviours can have mundane causes. **Susan** was increasingly distressed and aggressive. She has no verbal communication, and it was difficult to understand why she was so different to her usual self. She was also off her food and losing weight. There had been no recent changes in the people around her, or her routines. Careful examination revealed the need for extensive dental work. Once this was done she returned to her usual self.

People who support those with a learning disability are vital in alerting us to the possibility of a mental health problem. Their knowledge will clarify the change in a person's mood, thinking and behaviour. They can support a person to seek specialist advice. This is especially important when a person has limited communication skills. They can also assist in monitoring the effect of treatment. We need to know if an intervention is not working or is having unwanted effects, so that appropriate action is taken. Sometimes support staff may be asked to complete simple charts to help in this process.

Case study: James

I was asked to see **James** by his GP. James left school a year ago. Since then he had become increasingly sullen and bad tempered at home. He was not interested in doing things, such as playing his music. When I talked to James, he told me he was unhappy because he couldn't get a job or a girlfriend like other men his age. He felt his family did not understand him. I thought that James needed someone to talk his problems through with, and he agreed to see a counsellor. Together, they discussed how James might get closer to achieving what he wanted.

One day I was called to see James urgently as he had hit his mother for no apparent reason. He was very distressed, and unable to explain why he had done this. He then said he was hearing clicking in his head. I could not find a physical reason for this. I started James, with his agreement, on some tablets to remove what I supposed were hallucinations (clicking). Soon James was back to his usual self. He started some courses and began to see old friends again. James and I decided to see if he could manage without his tablets. Unfortunately, James began to feel miserable again and to hear 'noises in his head'. He asked to restart his tablets. We agreed to try to stop them again when he has been well for a year.

James continues to see a counsellor to find ways to be more positive in the way he thinks about himself and his changing role from that of a child to a more independent adult living in the family home. The help James is receiving aims to make him feel better and to cope differently in the future so that he is less likely to become ill again.

James was more ill than I had at first thought. I had viewed him as a young man understandably upset by what he saw as his lack of opportunities. Only later did I realise the depth of his distress, and that he was hearing sounds that no-one else could (hallucinations of clicking). When a person becomes mentally ill, normal feelings and thoughts may become more intense than usual and interfere with how they cope. This is what happens when someone has a **neurotic disorder**. I thought that James's sadness had reached this stage, and that he was neurotically depressed. Later I realised that James was to a degree out of touch with reality – he was having hallucinations – which is referred to as a **psychotic illness**.

There is no clear boundary between mental health and mental illness, or between neuroses and psychoses. There are many shades of grey in between, and of course our health changes from day-to-day. The approach we take to help a person depends on many things.

Treatment Throughout, James and I have talked about what we should do. For all of us it is important to give 'informed consent' to any treatment we have. This means that we understand what the treatment is, and what the effects of it might be. We also need to know what is likely to happen if we do not have the treatment. This does not only apply to medicines but also to other treatments, such as relaxation and counselling. James and I could talk together. It is more difficult to gain the view of someone with less verbal skills. However, wherever possible, a service user's consent to treatment should be sought. There are special procedures that need to be followed if this cannot happen, which will be specific to your organisation.

There are a variety of treatments available including different psychotherapies, medicines, relaxation and behavioural strategies. For James, a combination of counselling and medicine has worked well. For someone else, a different approach may be better.

Summary Those who support people with learning disabilities need to:

- promote positive mental health, for instance, by promoting relationships and active lifestyles

- be alert to the possibility that if a person is not their normal self there could be a variety of reasons, including mental illness

- be able to support people to access help

- assist in the implementation of treatments

- be able to monitor the effects of interventions.

Only by working together can the mental health needs of people with learning disabilities be met.

> **Further reading**
>
> Bouras, N. (1999) (Ed) *Psychiatric and Behavioural Disorders in Developmental Disabilities and Mental Retardation.* Cambridge: Cambridge Press.
>
> Hollins, S. & Curran, J. (1996) *Understanding Depression in People with Learning Disabilities: A training pack for staff and carers.* Brighton: Pavilion.
>
> O'Hara, J. & Sperlinger, A. (1997) Mental Health Needs. In: J. O'Hara and A. Sperlinger (Eds) *Learning Disabilities: A practical approach for health professionals.* Chichester: Wiley.
>
> Piachaud, J. (1999) Issues for mental health in learning disabilities services. *Tizard Learning Disability Review* **4** (2) 47–48.

Chapter 16

ISSUES ACROSS
THE LIFE PATH

KEY WORDS

control

predictability

involvement

loss

Managing change,
transition and loss

This chapter addresses some of the ways that people with
learning disabilities can be supported around times of transition
and loss. Major changes such as a move, a bereavement or the
beginning or ending of a significant relationship can be
emotionally taxing for anyone. For people who are marginalised
or who struggle with making sense of their world because of
limited communication skills or additional disabilities, managing
such major changes can be even more difficult.

This chapter makes reference to some practical ways in which
it is possible to reduce the confusion and emotional turmoil that
people with learning disabilities may experience at times of loss
and transition.

WRITTEN BY
Henrik Lynggaard

Harperbury Hospital is one of the many old 'mentally handicapped hospitals', and similar institutions, that has been torn down in the last 20 years. People with learning disabilities, some of whom had been living an institutionalised life since childhood, moved into the community.

Saying goodbye, saying hello Frequent changes can be a feature in the lives of many people with learning disabilities, not least when establishing and ending relationships with the staff who support them in day and residential settings. As many people with learning disabilities are dependent on carers to help meet their physical, social and emotional needs, the relationship between staff and service users can become very important. However, with a high turnover of staff, it is not uncommon for people with learning disabilities to regularly experience separation and loss when keyworkers with whom they have established a relationship move away. Mattison and Pistrang (2000) have written a thought-provoking and engaging account of a series of interviews with keyworkers and people with learning disabilities in residential homes about the experience of keyworkers leaving. They found that these separations were often far more emotionally significant for people with learning disabilities than many of the staff had imagined.

'Care staff may devalue their own role in clients' lives, perhaps partly because the staff themselves are not valued within the service where they work. For keyworkers who do recognise the importance of their role, it can be hard to tolerate the responsibility and guilt of leaving. This in turn may make it difficult to acknowledge or attend to the client's feelings of loss.'

All the residents who were interviewed about endings said that they much preferred to be given plenty of notice about the departure of their keyworker so that they could prepare themselves better. Their preference echoes conclusions made in other studies that have shown that helping people with learning disabilities to anticipate and plan for endings can significantly reduce the impact of loss (Siebold, 1991).

Anticipating and planning endings may take many forms, and will to some degree be determined by the individual's level of functioning. However, an important part of managing change involves finding accessible and meaningful ways of informing people with learning disabilities about events that affect them, such as the departure of significant people in their lives. This is a task that should not just be left to the individual workers leaving but also requires the active involvement and contributions of those who remain. Staff who remain may need to reinforce a message that the person has left and may find themselves having important conversations with the person with learning disabilities about the staff member who left.

Many of us who have worked closely with people with learning disabilities will at some time or other have found ourselves, at the point of saying goodbye, making vague promises about keeping in touch, as a way of easing the pain of leaving. Studies and experience show that, while well intentioned, this generally proves unhelpful to the person leaving, the person left behind and to the staff who come after.

The **process of saying goodbye** is, of course, about more than the sadness that endings often evoke. It can also involve **reviewing memories** of times spent together and things that have been accomplished. The use of photos, drawings, objects, sensory experiences and words may all facilitate this task. Additionally, **the marking of endings can act as the bridge to the future**, to **new opportunities** and new relationships. New keyworkers may bring **new understandings**, and may act as facilitators of **new developments**.

Attending to **how new people are received and welcomed** into services is just as important as thinking about endings. Preparation for the arrival of a new person in a service can significantly shape the success or failure of the experience for all concerned. This preparation is equally important whether the 'new' person is a new tenant with learning disabilities, or a new member of staff joining the support team. (We see this from Sonia's example on page 216, which provides details about some of the preparations for a resident's move to a new home.)

Transitions

Change is both an important and inevitable part of growth and development. Whether changes are **positive** (eg a job promotion, a move to better accommodation) or **negative** (eg the sudden end of a relationship, the diagnosis of an illness), they trigger reactions and require a period of adjustment. Studies of the effect of transitions have shown that **transitions are most stressful if they are:**

- **unpredictable** (eg the sudden closure of a residential home)

- **involuntary** (eg the relocation of one's place of work)

- **unfamiliar** (eg moving to a setting where different rules apply or a different language is spoken)

- of **high intensity and frequency** (Hopson, 1981).

By contrast, research into successful outcomes of transition has shown that, amongst other things, they depend on:

- **involvement** of the people affected

- **predictability** of the event (even if potentially stressful)

- whether the person has **control** over the duration of the transition

- availability of **social support** (Kobasa *et al*, 1982).

People with learning disabilities are often subject to many changes and transitions over which they have little or no control, choice or involvement. Research has shown that where people are not involved or consulted about major moves and transitions they fare much worse psychologically when compared to groups of people who have been involved in meaningful ways, who have received relevant and accessible information, and where careful planning has taken place (see, for example, Collins, 1994).

Moving to a new home is often rated as one of the most stressful events in many stress indexes, even if the move may eventually lead to many positive changes. Below is an example of some of the ways that Sonia was supported to move to a new home in another part of the country.

Case study: Sonia

Sonia, who had a diagnosis of autism and a severe learning disability, needed to move on when the home in which she was living was closing down. The staff who had worked with Sonia over many years knew that she struggled with understanding references to things that might happen in the future, and that she became anxious when things were uncertain and vague. In Sonia's case they felt that she would manage a relatively short transition period best and that they would support her to make sense of what was happening by drawing on her interest in looking at photographs. Once they had received a firm guarantee that Sonia's new home was ready for her, a date was set for her move and the work of helping Sonia to understand what was happening began. The staff team's insistence on having absolute assurance of the moving date was based on their experience of managing all the additional confusion and distress that may arise when delays occur such as building works overrunning or other residents not moving out.

Case study: Sonia *(cont.)…*

With the moving date established, staff at Sonia's old and new homes could engage in supporting her move. First, Sonia went on a visit with members of staff to her new home. She indicated that she liked her new environment with its safe open spaces, and many photos were taken of Sonia in her new home. Returning home these photographs were developed and served as an aid for staff to start talking with Sonia about the move. Staff from Sonia's new home worked alongside her old staff team for several shifts in order to learn about some of the more subtle ways of supporting her that were not always easy to capture in written notes and reports.

During Sonia's last week in her old home, a very large calendar with the numbers from 1 to 7 was displayed on the wall in her home. Next to the last number in the calendar a photo of Sonia outside her new home appeared. Pictures were also stuck beside some of the other numbers in the 'count-down calendar'. There were pictures that helped Sonia to understand that: three days before her move she would be going to a local restaurant where she had enjoyed many meals and been made to feel welcome by the owners; two days before she moved there would be a leaving party for her; on the day before she moved pictures of bags and suitcases indicated that she would be packing her things with her keyworker etc. At the end of every day Sonia and a member of staff used a big red pen to cross out one of the days to signal the progressive count-down.

Sonia also had a large collection of photos she took with her to her new home. The staff had remembered to date the photos and to write on the back who was in the picture and their relationship to Sonia. The staff were mindful that without such details people who worked with Sonia in years to come would not be able to talk to her about all the people and places that had been important to her.

Bereavement A few weeks before the planned start of a group for people with learning disabilities who had lost a parent, I received a short letter from **Paul**'s main carer. She wrote…

'I don't want Paul to attend your meetings. He doesn't understand death and never will. It is a year since his Dad died and he has accepted that he isn't coming home anymore. He isn't at all upset and is his happy self. My Doctor agrees with me to leave things as they are.'

In a few lines, Paul's carer succinctly expresses many of the views and beliefs that have informed responses to people with learning disabilities when they lose a significant person in their life. Historically, it has often been assumed that people with learning disabilities are unable to develop strong attachments and close relationships that are likely to result in feelings of personal loss, and that they therefore do not experience grief (Oswin, 1991;

Mattison & Pistrang, 2000). Some of the results of these beliefs and assumptions have been:

1   **To overlook grief reactions, or to mislabel them as challenging behaviour** (Emerson, 1977). Hollins and Esterhuyzen (1997) followed 50 people with learning disabilities who had lost a parent and compared them with another group of 50 learning disabled people who had not been bereaved. They found that there was a much higher rate of behavioural and emotional difficulties in the bereaved group compared with the non-bereaved group. In the case of Paul for instance, whilst he might have been his happy self at home, the situation at the day centre was very different. There he was tearful and had become very attached to his male keyworker whom he rarely let out of his sight.

2   **To neglect giving clear explanations or to use confusing euphemisms to refer to death.** This was illustrated in Paul's case where his father's death was referred to as '*him not coming home anymore*'.

3   **To rush people with learning disability into institutional care, with little or no explanation, when a main carer dies.** This intervention often removes them from all that is familiar and that gives meaning to their experience (Oswin, 1991).

4   **To exclude people from the social responses and rituals associated with death.** Hollins and Esterhuyzen's research showed that only about half of the bereaved people had been involved in any of the social responses associated with death, such as a funeral.

Studies have indicated that it is indeed possible for people with learning disabilities to understand death and loss (McEvoy, 1987) and that it is important not to assume that a person does not feel any grief because he or she cannot verbally express it (Oswin, 1991).

For example: Paul, who had very limited speech, was able to communicate his distress and confusion through his behaviour at the day centre where he demonstrated his fear that another important male figure in his life, his keyworker, might disappear.

As is the case among people *without* learning disabilities, reactions can vary widely and depend on many factors. These might include:

- the nature of the relationship with the person who has died

- the circumstances of death (sudden or unexpected)

- the history of previous losses and how these were resolved.

Sometimes, reactions may be delayed or a current loss may evoke previous ones.

There are many ways of supporting people who are experiencing or have experienced a loss, and there will be many factors that will influence what is and is not appropriate in particular circumstances. Listed opposite are some ideas and suggestions, and many others could be added. It is important to remember that **each person with a learning disability is an individual and will grieve as an individual**, although cultural belief systems are likely to play an important part in shaping the way that grief is manifested and expressed.

Working with people before a death

- Create opportunities to talk and check the person's understanding about what is happening.

- Use clear and unambiguous language.

- Have death and dying on the agenda. Use opportune moments; for example, death of characters in soap operas on TV, stories of people or pets who have died etc as reference points.

- Get a sense of the person's bereavement history (family members, friends who have died). How were they involved, how did they react?

- Where appropriate, discuss the person's own thoughts about death and acknowledge any anxieties they may have.

- Familiarise people with the idea of funerals, cremations or other ceremonies using visits or resource booklets.

Working with people following a death

- Be open about the death (circumstances and causes).

- Avoid confusing euphemisms ('not coming home anymore'; 'gone to sleep' etc).

- Talk about the person who has died; explore memories.

- Many media such as photographs, drawings, life story books, mementoes, booklets can be used to facilitate discussions.

- Encourage attendance at funerals, memorials, and culturally appropriate rituals etc, and, where appropriate, seek to involve the person in meaningful ways (eg sharing memories about the person who has died).

- Be aware that bereavement reactions may be delayed, or may be triggered by other losses (eg the departure of a keyworker, or moving house).

- Ongoing support is important – be aware of anniversaries and special festivals (eg Christmas, birthdays or other festivals).

Guidelines for support

The following are some areas to consider where the death of someone close to an individual with learning disabilities is expected and may also be incorporated into working practices in day centres and residential homes. **Being proactive in thinking about, and planning for, death can reduce the impact of loss (Siebold, 1991) and facilitate the way that grief is processed.**

Resources

The past 10 to 15 years have seen the publication of an increasing range of resources about death and bereavement that can be used to facilitate conversation with people with learning disabilities who have experienced a loss. Many of these resources are in the form of colourful booklets, flashcards and videos and can be used with people with few verbal skills. Easily accessible books have also been written for carers and staff groups.

Cathcart, F. (1994) *Understanding Death and Dying*. A series of three booklets for the user, relative and professional carer. Available from the British Institute of Learning Disabilities.

Cooley, J. & McGauran, F. (2001) *Talking Together About Death*. London: Winslow Press.

Hollins, S. & Sireling, L. (1989) *When Dad Died* and *When Mum Died*. Books Without Words series. London: Royal College of Psychiatrists.

Watchman, K. (2001) *Let's Talk About Death: A booklet about death and funerals for adults who have a learning disability*. Available from the Scottish Down's Syndrome Association.

Further reading

Collins, J. (1994) *Still To Be Settled: Strategies for the resettlement of people from mental handicap hospitals.* London: Values into Action.

Hollins, S. & Esterhuyzen, A. (1997) Bereavement and grief in adults with learning disabilities. *British Journal of Psychiatry* **170** 497–501.

Hopson, B. (1981) Transition: Understanding and managing personal change. In: M. Herbert (Ed) *Psychology for Social Workers.* London: Macmillan.

Oswin, M. (1991) *Am I Allowed to Cry? A study of bereavement amongst people with learning difficulties.* Human Horizon Series.

References

Emerson, P. (1977) Covert grief reaction in mentally retarded clients. *Mental Retardation* **15** 46–7.

Kobasa, S. C., Madd, S. R. & Kahn, S. (1982). Hardness and health: A prospective study. *Journal of Personality and Social Psychology* **42** 168–177.

McEvoy, J. (1989) Investigating the concept of death in adults who are mentally handicapped. *British Journal of Mental Subnormality* **25** 115–121.

Mattison, V. & Pistrang, N. (2000) *Saying Goodbye: When keyworker relationships end.* London: Free Association Books.

Siebold, C. (1991) Termination: When the therapist leaves. *Clinical Social Work Journal* **19** 191–204.

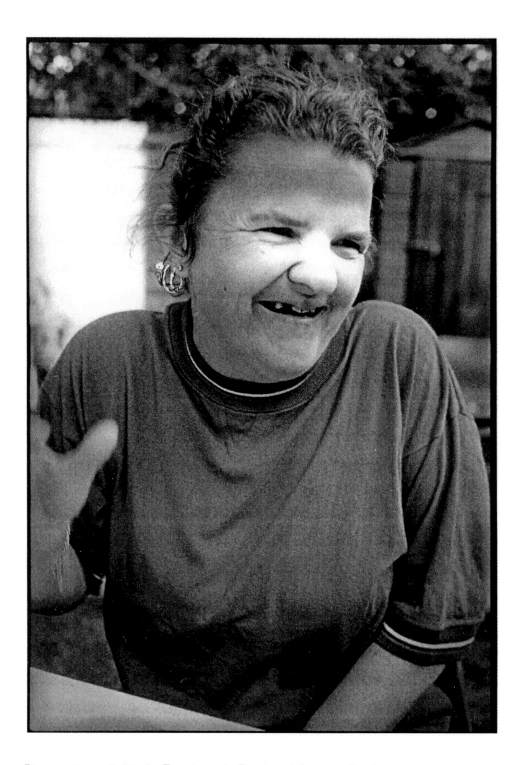

Photograph supplied by the Foundation for People with Learning Disabilities

WRITTEN BY
Annette McDonald

Chapter 17

NOT AS YOUNG AS WE USED TO BE

KEY WORDS

choice

community

diversity

experience

independence

longevity

quality in ageing

Supporting older people with learning disabilities

The general population in Britain is ageing. It is an issue that has raised much debate, especially with regard to what this increase in the number of older people implies for those with responsibility for providing health and social care. This debate has now crossed over into the field of learning disability. It is recognised that people with learning disabilities are also living longer, many of the present generation reaching the age of 60+, and yet there is little consensus in terms of the 'right' kind of service to offer this emerging group of people.

This chapter provides an outline of what is known about older people with learning disabilities, and suggests an agenda for those providing services. It makes reference to both the appropriateness of services for people with learning disabilities and services for older people in relation to those who are now growing older within the current learning disability service provision. It looks at the importance of training, specifically in the effects and impacts of the ageing process, and finally, it highlights some of the key issues for good practice.

Older people with learning disabilities: what do we know?

With this newly emerging client group it is fair to say that we know very little. It has been a commonly held belief that people with learning disabilities do not grow old, either in body or in mind, and it seems that services have been unprepared for this inevitability. As with the general population, advances in medical technology have led to improved longevity, and specific advances in perinatal care have led to children with profound and multiple disabilities surviving well beyond the first year of life.

- In the US, it is predicted that 40% of people with learning disabilities will live to the age of 60, and that 12% will be aged 65+.

- In Britain it was estimated (1991) that 47% of people with learning disabilities were aged over 45, and 17% were over 65. The estimated prevalence rate of over 60s per 1000 of the British population is between 0.4% and 0.5%.

- It is expected that mortality rates for people with learning disabilities will soon approach those of the general population, taking into account that **people with Down's Syndrome** have a **lower life expectancy** than other people with learning disabilities.

- As with the general population, it is expected that **women**, specifically those with mild learning disabilities living in the community, will have the **longest life expectancy**.

- As yet there are no conclusive figures regarding the expected prevalence of older people with learning disabilities from **minority ethnic communities**. However, studies already indicate that the prevalence of learning disabilities among black and ethnic minority children is higher than among white children (Baxter *et al*, 1990). There is no reason to assume that life expectancy among minority ethnic communities will be any lower than that of the white population.

Ageing family carers

A large number of people with learning disabilities currently live with their parents or carers, and it is increasingly acknowledged that they are outliving them. In addition older people with learning disabilities were among the last to leave the large institutions. The adaptation – and indeed the acceptance of people's ability to adapt to community living after so many years of institutional or home care and at a greater age – must pose as yet unidentified difficulties for some individuals. The potential of older people with learning disabilities has been greatly underestimated, and this has led to marginalisation, limited choices and care options.

Current service provision: how appropriate is it as people grow older?

What do we know?

As with any other group of people in society, we cannot talk about older people with learning disabilities as if they all share the same traits and characteristics, whether those characteristics are associated with learning disability or with older age. The diversity and unique 'personhood' of individuals continue throughout the lifespan, and the diversity of the learning disabled population suggests that a range of services and responses is required to serve the needs of the older people among them. Little is known about the physical, psychological, emotional and social processes of ageing among people with learning disabilities, and as yet the consequences of old age for people with learning disabilities, their families, carers and service providers are unknown.

Tailoring services

In recognition of the size of the ageing general population there has been a move toward encouraging preparation for self-sufficiency in older age. This includes the provision of personal pensions and medical plans, financial savings and purchase of property to cover the cost of residential or nursing home care in later life. The range and spectrum of services available for older people is gradually increasing. It is no longer assumed that older people are simply 'put out to pasture' in old people's homes, but can be offered home care in the community and minimum or extra-care sheltered housing in addition to the more traditional residential services or long-stay hospital wards.

It is also beginning to be recognised that older people have specific needs related to the maintenance of personhood, inclusion, purpose, companionship and the psychological and physical changes associated with ageing. Older people with learning disabilities will have had little opportunity to provide

Photograph supplied by the Foundation for People with Learning Disabilities

for their old age. For many, state benefits will have been their only income, and the purchase of property well beyond their means. In an increasingly materialistic society this can only limit the choice of future service options available for them within current older persons provision, and this raises the question of whether a comprehensive range of specialist services should be developed.

Special or normal?

Services are fragmented into different specialisms. **Service assumptions for older people can often be restricting and disempowering** – but service philosophy for people with learning disabilities advocates **integration**. How advantageous will *continued* integration be if there is no awareness or understanding of the specific needs of people with learning disabilities among the staff and existing users of available services for older people?

Just as this premise applies to older persons' services, it can also apply to services for people with learning disabilities. How appropriate are the principles of 'normalisation' and the attainment of the Five Service Accomplishments (eg O'Brien & Tyne, 1981), when traditionally perceived 'normal' and 'valued' lifestyles for older people may not include a desire to be actively integrated into society? After all, many older people are keener to quietly retire into a familiar environment, where the emphasis is on being cared for, and not being supported to independence.

Applying service principles to older people with learning disabilities has inherent difficulties, according to Wolfensberger (1985), and unless there is policy recognition of the particular problems facing older people with learning disabilities there is a danger of 'double jeopardy'. They are likely to be poorly served by both sets of services – those for older people *and* those for people with learning disabilities.

The Providers Agenda: policy recognition and service development

In a key study of Community Care Plans, Robertson *et al* (1996) found that only 33% made mention of older people with learning disabilities. Even though service managers were acutely aware of the need for policy and service development, few areas had worked towards this, and different areas were responding differently to both actual and potential demand. There was evidence that older people with learning disabilities were beginning to be recognised as a specific user group, but the task of providing services for them is difficult.

Service planners and providers need to balance two objectives and provide an accessible range of services that respond both:

- to the diverse, age-related needs and difficulties faced by older people with learning disabilities

- to the psychological, physical, emotional and social needs associated with the ageing process.

There is a need to **maintain autonomy** and the **potential for making choices**, **to sustain close personal relationships** and **enable** full use of leisure time for the individual with learning disabilities. There is also a need to see the older person in the context of their whole-life experience and unique personhood. The challenge, therefore, is to **respect autonomy, diversity and individuality**, whilst providing **additional supports** where needed with respect to the process of growing older.

Policies for people with learning disabilities have failed to consider the dimension of ageing, even though studies have long recognised the high incidence of disability in older age. Compared to the general population, older people with learning disabilities have a higher prevalence of psychological and physical disorders, and it is to be assumed that they will not be immune to the illnesses and the mental and physical decline associated with the ageing process. Indeed, **people with Down's Syndrome have a higher potential for developing Alzheimer's-related dementia**.

Planning services

Great diversity in terms of provision models has led to little consensus in terms of the 'right' kind of service to offer older people with learning disabilities, and this has restricted any kind of universality of approach. In planning appropriate services it is vital to take into account:

- the size of the local population
- *actual*, as well as perceived, need
- physical and mental health care needs, specifically in relation to dementia
- social care needs, and age-associated community links
- accessible housing, providing security within a familiar and adaptable environment
- interagency collaboration and access to community health and social services
- a spectrum of services ranging from domiciliary care *in situ* to nursing home care
- the needs of family and informal carers.

The importance of training: sharing cross-agency experience and skills

Just as services are fragmented into specialisms, so too is training. There is a tendency to limit the scope of training to a specific user group, and little time is set aside to explore both the variances and commonalities associated with the lives of people with differing disabilities within that specific grouping. The term 'dual diagnosis' appears to be commonly accepted but is also given many divergent definitions. The implications of 'dual diagnosis' are never truly explored. This seems especially true in relation to individual lifestyle and the process of ageing, although there is no evidence to suggest that this experience will be any different – or less individual – for people with disabilities than it will be for people in the general population.

There is a great need within current services for people with learning disabilities for training in anti-ageist practice, in order to prevent discriminatory working practices and to recognise and positively acknowledge the changes inherent in the ageing process. There is a need for training in **lifespan issues** (such as moving from a family home, retirement, bereavement, loss of memory and changes in physical and mental health) which can only assist the effective support of older people with learning disabilities as they experience critical transitions. There is also scope for training in **reminiscence**, **personal biography** and **life review therapy**.

'There is no method of therapeutic practice that cannot be applied to work with older people provided, as with clients of other ages, the method selected is appropriate to the abilities and wishes of the user, the experience of the worker and the nature of the identified problem.'
(Hughes, 1995)

Access to training

It should not be necessary to look far for this training; there is a wealth of it among the current specialisms, and this existing knowledge can simply be adapted and applied to the specific issue of older people with learning disabilities. The key lies in interagency collaboration, joint working and the sharing of existing experience, skills and knowledge.

Summary   **Suggested principles of good practice for supporting older people with learning disabilities**

- Identify, as well as predict, actual as well as perceived future need, specifically with reference to accessible housing, social and health care needs.

- Consider the appropriateness of existing service provision, both for people with learning disabilities and for older people, and identify service deficit in both areas with relation to older people with learning disabilities.

- Consider ageing *in situ*, environmental adaptation, and the development of specialist domiciliary care agencies.

- Map and develop community links, and routes of access to health, housing and social services.

- Develop staff training, specifically in the areas of anti-ageist practice and positive awareness of the ageing process.

- Recognise the quality of family care and consult the carers.

- Recognise the heterogeneity and unique personhood of the older people with learning disabilities, and tailor service provision through the individual planning process.

- Involve older service users with learning disabilities in service planning, in ways appropriate to their understanding, interest and motivation.

- Positively encourage interagency collaboration, joint working and the sharing of existing experience, skills and knowledge.

Further reading

Felce, D. & Murphy, G. (2001) *Journal of Applied Research in Intellelctual Disability Research – Special edition on ageing and intellectual disabilities* (various contributors) **14** (3).

Harris, J., Bennett, L., Hogg, J. & Moss, S. (1997) *Ageing Matters: Pathways for older people with a learning disability.* Independent study materials.

Lambe, L., Hogg, J. & Moss, S. (1998) *Ageing Matters: Pathways for older people with a learning disability.* Resource Pack. Kidderminster: BILD.

Moss, S. C. (1994) Quality of Life and Ageing. In: D. A. Goode (Ed) *Quality of Life for Persons with Disabilities: International perspectives and issues.* Cambridge, MA: Brookline Books.

References

Baxter, C., Poonia, K., Ward, L. & Nadirshaw, Z. (1990) *Double Discrimination: Issues and services for people with learning disabilities from black and ethnic minority communities.* London: King's Fund.

Hughes, B. (1995) *Older People and Community Care: Critical theory and practice.* Buckingham: Open University Press.

O'Brien, J. & Tyne, A. (1981) *The Principle of Normalisation: A foundation for effective services.* London: Campaign for Mentally Handicapped People: Community and Mental Handicap Educational and Research Association.

Wolfensberger, W. (1983) *Reflections on the Status of Citizen Advocacy.* Toronto: National Institute of Mental Retardation.

 # Glossary

advocacy

self-advocacy	speaking out for, or representing, expressing yourself and your views/needs etc
peer advocacy	being supported by someone else who shares or has shared a similar experience, or role, to you
citizen advocacy	having your views or perspective represented by someone from your community
Antecedent Behaviour Consequences (ABC)	a framework for studying challenging behaviour that involves recording the events that lead up to an incident (A), the nature of the incident itself (B) and the events that follow (C)
anti-oppressive practice	practice that does not make any assumptions about, exceptions for, or giving special treatment to someone you are caring for, just because of their colour, gender, sexuality etc
assessment	considering many different aspects of an individual and their situation, in order to make decisions about the kind of care they need
block treatment	treating many people in the same way (as opposed to looking at each individual and finding the most appropriate treatment for their specific needs)

communication	sharing information, expressing ideas, thoughts, feelings and desires to another person, by some means eg speaking, writing down, using sounds etc
augmented/augmentative communication	the use of a range of communication methods in addition to speech, such as eye contact, signing, symbol and picture charts and electronic aids
communication barriers	inappropriate or non-existent adaptation in the social communication environment which inhibits the person's use of available communication skills
communication environment	the place where communication takes place
communication partnership	the significant people in the individual's life with whom communication takes place; this is influenced by the relationship, knowledge, experience, attitude and cultural identity of the participants
communication ramp	much like a wheelchair ramp, a communication ramp offers support to a person who is trying to communicate, and presents them with a tool/way to overcome or work around the barriers. Communication ramps are used to promote skills use by the person with a learning disability and include all forms of alternative and augmentative communication. Examples include: using simple language; gesture; signs; objects of reference; pointing; pictures and symbols; communicating at a slower pace; guessing what a person's behaviour means and checking out an interpretation, etc.

communication skills	the communication strengths of an individual or the skills that they are able to use, whether they involve the use of *conventional linguistic code* eg speech or *non-conventional communication behaviour* eg eye gaze, vocalisation, body language, etc.
consensus	general agreement; majority view
consent (to give consent)	to express willingness; give permission; be compliant to another's suggestion. The important aspect of consent in learning disabilities is ensuring that someone is able to fully understand what is being suggested before they can give **informed consent**
containment	**1.** keeping everyone in the same place **2.** containing, or controlling difficulties rather than taking active steps to solve or improve them
control	exerting power over actions, either your own, or those of other people; taking the lead
demand avoidance	the act of behaving in ways that avoid demands placed on you by others eg the person self-injuring when people ask them to wash the dishes
depersonalisation	not seeing people as individuals, but as numbers/labels etc. This can happen in a number of ways: either because we do not perceive people with learning disabilities to be as human as we are, and therefore do not treat them as individuals, by taking away those elements of a person that make them individuals
	– making choices, from choosing clothes to choosing where to live

	– pursuing dreams and goals, including hobbies, such as playing football, or painting etc
	– having those choices respected and supported
discrimination	making distinctions about people, treating someone in a different way because of their colour, race, gender, sexuality etc, and acting differently towards them on the basis of assumptions made as a result
empowerment	the act of supporting or enabling power for/with those who have no, or little, power/control in their lives
equitable	fair, just
evaluation	informed, stated (clinical) judgement(s) (follows **assessment**)
exploit, exploited, exploitation	take advantage of, use for your own purposes
external factors	something which affects a situation from the outside eg a day centre's activities might be affected by a change in national law
gender	a culturally shaped group of attributes and behaviours assigned to the male or female. Therefore, a gender difference is that women (rather than men) usually look after children
gender-blind	this term describes someone or something that does not take the sex of a person into account when making a decision
generic	general, not specific, typical/average/all encompassing
heterogeneity	variety, diversity

heterosexism	a belief that heterosexuality is more normal, more morally right than homosexuality
heterosexual	sexually attracted to the opposite sex
homophobia	an irrational fear or disgust of lesbians and gay men
impairment	a difficulty, or 'physical inefficiency' which prevents or reduces the effectiveness of some capability eg 'hearing impaired' would now be used to describe someone who has difficulty hearing
implementation	putting something into practice; the turning of an idea into action
infantilisation	making someone seem like a child/infant. This might be done by, for example, dressing someone in clothes that are inappropriate to their age
informed risk-taking (see also **risk assessment**)	making decisions to carry out actions or activities, but only after having considered the potential risks involved
inter	from the Latin meaning 'between'
interaction, interactive	the 'give and take' between people who are sharing activities and conversation
intermediary	a person who works between two parties, or people. Someone who carries ideas and messages from one person to the other. (Literally means 'between a middle way' and can have the meaning of a kind of diplomat)
internal factors	something which affects a situation from the inside eg a day centre's activities might be affected by a staff member leaving

longevity	long life
lucidity	clear expression, easy to understand
neglect	fail to care for, disregard, lack of caring
non-verbal behaviours	all means of communication other than spoken words eg eye gaze, intonation etc
oppression	prolonged or harsh or cruel treatment or control
person-centred	*as it sounds;* in care circles, it describes care which is focused on, and provided for, the person being cared for, rather than the preferences or convenience of the carer or organisation
positive prevention strategies	actively seeking to stop difficulties from arising, rather than a more passive practice that deals with difficulties when they arise
practitioners	people carrying out, or providing care
predictability	how likely or unlikely something is
predisposing factors	situations, people, circumstances etc which make an outcome more likely to happen eg it is more likely that Jack will become anxious if he is not told in advance that he is about to eat
prevalence	existence
punitive	used to describe actions/practice ie punishing, or meant to upset or hurt (usually emotionally)
risk assessment	careful consideration of the level or presence of danger or difficulty eg working out whether it is safe for the individual and caring staff to take someone to a football match (see **risk management**, below)

risk management	taking steps to reduce danger or difficulties which you have identified as being possible in a situation eg (see above) making sure that you have enough staff and any medication necessary to deal with an individual who may have an epileptic fit when at that football match
self-stimulation	inducing a physical sensation on oneself eg an individual who does not experience physical contact, hugging etc may bang their head, in order that they experience physical sensation
sensory disabilities	a difficulty or deficiency of one of the five senses – sight, hearing, touch, taste or smell
sex	the biology of a person, whether they are female or male. Therefore a sex difference is that women give birth to children
sexuality	the organisation, expression and direction of sexual desire, love, loyalty, passion, affection, intimacy
sexual identity	a sense of one's own sexuality
sexual orientation	a natural inclination towards a particular sexual identity
significant	when describing disability, it means substantial, requiring more consideration and specialised care
significant others	other important people
social exclusion	rejected by, or not included in, society as a whole, not considered 'normal', not 'fitting'; outside of, or unable to access, social basics – jobs, housing, services etc

social functioning	the manner in which we act and interact with other people in society, in approved or appropriate ways
social isolation	being within society but not connected to it. For example, being eligible for, but unaware of, services designed to help you
stigmatise	describe in a negative, and distasteful manner; apply negative characteristics to something eg mental illness is often regarded as a stigma as media often describes it in violent terms
terminology	jargon
total communication	the use of all available and appropriate means to communicate – eye gaze, body language, facial expression, gestures, signs, symbols, voice and speech; demonstration of what needs doing, pointing to or using things available in the environment
transaction	an exchange; in the sense of communication it is an exchange of feelings, information or ideas
victimisation	making someone into a victim; focused, cruel treatment of someone which is unfair
vocalisation	making a noise using one's voice

 # Available from Pavilion

Publications

Creative Arts and People with Profound and Multiple Learning Disabilities
Innovative practices to broaden the experiences of people with profound and multiple learning disabilities

LORETTO LAMB AND JAMES HOGG

'*…extremely informative, realistic and flexible in its approach and invaluable as a resource itself*'
The Frontline in Learning Disability

Creative arts offer an important leisure activity for people with profound and multiple learning disabilities. This handbook draws together innovative work and practice, explaining how to extend the boundaries of experience for people with profound disabilities. Based on respected education, therapy and leisure practices, the book presents four main areas of activity: sensory experience, visual arts, experiencing and making music and the performing arts.

Packed with activities, the manual provides a compendium of resources to help find activities that are of value to those people with profound and multiple disabilities.

Of particular interest to: family and carers, teachers, day service staff, therapists, voluntary organisations, community arts and leisure providers, specialists in leisure provision.

Format: A4 manual (82pp).

Published by Pavilion

£39.95   Order Code 58P   ISBN:1 84196 020 9

Keyworking

A training resource pack on keyworking and the role of the professional keyworker

JENNY PEARCE WITH SHELLEY SMITH

This training pack, which has been developed by Elizabeth FitzRoy Homes, offers everything you need to run a one-day course on the role and responsibilities of a professional keyworker – the carer who develops a relationship with a specific individual, deals with their care and acts as their advocate.

Of particular interest to: support workers, staff who have the role of keyworker and staff who support or supervise keyworkers.

Format: ringbound training materials (120pp) including trainer's notes incorporating OHP masters and handouts.

£75   Order Code 57P   ISBN: 1 841960 21 7

This is My Home

Challenging the language of care and control

Drawing on the results of previous research into tenant satisfaction, this video resource has been designed for all those who live and work in supported housing.

This is My Home focuses on the significance of language and control in the process of empowerment. It illustrates how people can explore the language currently used within their service to decide whether it affects them positively or negatively.

The video is suitable for use with groups of staff and tenants with a wide range of needs and shows how people with few or no verbal communication skills can be encouraged to make choices about how and where they live.

Accompanying notes encourage discussion and positive action planning. The resource may be used for both staff training and group training for workers and tenants together.

Produced for the Joseph Rowntree Foundation by Pavilion in collaboration with Advocacy in Action and the Notting Hill Housing Trust.

Format: video (26 mins), notes 6pp.

£30 plus VAT (total £35.25)   Order Code 56D

Special price for self-advocacy and service-user groups: £15 plus VAT

Room To Move

Helping families look at the practical and emotional issues involved when young people with learning disabilities decide to leave home

Room To Move looks at the issues involved when a young person wishes to live independently of their family. It will help families consider the process in several stages:

- The initial discussions about the young person moving
- Planning the move
- Timing of the move
- Immediately after the move
- The long term.

There are practical tips for parents and views of the young people themselves showing how they cope with the move and the new situation. Tools within the handbook are included to help keep the young people at the centre of this decision-making process.

This video pack is of particular interest: to parents of young people with learning disabilities and staff and managers who are working with families and young people making the transition from home to independent living.

Format: A5 booklet (100pp) and video.

Published by Pavilion for the Joseph Rowntree Foundation

Complete Set (Including Handbook): £45 + VAT (Total £52.87) Order Code 41E

Handbook (available separately)

£15.95   Order Code 79D   ISBN: 1 84196 009 8

*Subsidised by JRF

You Don't Know What It's Like

Ways of building relationships with people who have autism and other communication difficulties

PHOEBE CALDWELL AND MATT HOGHTON

In this new resource the respected author Phoebe Caldwell draws upon her personal experience to illustrate methods of communication and to help readers set aside their reality. This enables them to enter the worlds of others who are struggling to interpret and respond to sets of sensory perceptions different to those we experience in our 'normal' world. The key approach is to work creatively, based on an understanding of what a person is experiencing and what it is their behaviour is trying to tell us. The text helps the reader to ask the question: What messages is an individual getting from the world they live in? Which of these has meaning for them? Which of these do they perceive as scary and is this leading them to behave as they do? Can we meet their needs? If not, can we modify their environment?

This handbook is invaluable to all those working with people with autistic spectrum disorder and behavioural challenges.

Format: A4 handbook (60pp).

Published by Pavilion

£25   Order Code 64P   ISBN: 1 84196 023 2

Person To Person

Establishing contact and communication with people with profound disabilities or whose behaviour is challenging

PHOEBE CALDWELL WITH PENE STEVENS

Expanding upon the approach introduced in *Getting In Touch*, this handbook emphasises the importance of developing a two-way relationship with individuals who have profound disabilities, whether they are autistic or present behaviour experienced as challenging. This fascinating, practical guide will be of help to staff who wish to become more proactive in enhancing the lives of people with learning disabilities by using their own language or familiar stimuli.

Format: A4 manual (90pp).

Published by Pavilion

£19.95   Order Code 31P   ISBN: 1 900600 43 9

Going With The Flow

Kirsten Stalker, Paul Duckett and Murna Downs

Just like the rest of the population, people with learning difficulties are living longer and are joining the growing number of individuals diagnosed with dementia. This report will improve the understanding of the needs of people with learning disabilities and dementia and provide a basis for improving existing services (48pp).

£10.95   Order Code 64D   ISBN: 1 84196 04 7

To order any of the above publications call our customer service team on: 01273 623222 or order online: www.pavpub.com

250

Journals

Tizard Learning Disability Review Journal

The *Tizard Learning Disability Review* is the leading journal providing the highest quality source of information for all professionals in the field. The Review identifies the practical outcomes from research and provides excellent coverage of current policy and practice issues in a focused and informative manner. Through peer-reviewed contributions the journal aims to bridge experiences, establishing a constructive dialogue between the different perspectives, from carers to managers, practitioners and academics.

The journal is published quarterly. For more details on subscribing please contact our customer services team on 01273 623222.

Living WELL Journal

Launched in 2001, *Living WELL* is a new journal which aims to promote better quality lifestyles for people with learning difficulties. Its unique focus on good practice in WORK, EDUCATION, LEISURE and LIFESTYLE, as the acronym suggests, will help subscribers work towards genuinely inclusive connections and relationships in the community. Each issue is full of inspiring features in an accessible format with a common-sense approach that readers can use to maintain and develop good practice within their own agency.

The journal is published quarterly. For more details on subscribing please contact ourcustomer services team on 01273 623222.

Available from the Foundation for People with Learning Disabilities

Learning Disabilities: The Fundamental Facts

PROFESSOR ERIC EMERSON, DR CHRIS HATTON,
PROFESSOR DAVID FELCE AND PROFESSOR GLYNIS MURPHY

This major new title is an extensive summary of learning disability research, providing a unique handbook of key facts and figures. It is the most comprehensive compilation and analysis available, covering all the key areas of learning disability.

Key themes

- Examines the latest research about developments in service provision

- Contains sections of the additional needs of people with learning disability, including health needs, sensory impairment, communication, and mental health.

- Examines the cost of service provision and current levels of spending.

- Records the unacceptable. Research has shown the bullying is an everyday experience for people with learning disabilities.

- Provides key definitions and background into causes of learning disabilities.

Published by the Foundation for People with Learning Disabilities

£22.50 P&P 10%   ISBN: 0 901944 98X   56 pp

Everyday Lives, Everyday Choices

For people with learning disabilities and high support needs

This report is the outcome of the Choice Initiative. This Initiative funded five innovative projects looking at the obstacles to communication and choice for people with high support needs. *Everyday Lives, Everyday Choices* consists of contributions from experts in the field alongside the experiences of the projects. The key themes of the report are: communication as the essential starting point in addressing choice, the role of citizen advocacy, and choice in employment, community activities and friendship. The report also includes chapters on the creative management of risk and choice, and staff development and training.

Everyday Lives, Everyday Choices demonstrates conclusively that choice is of real importance to people with high support needs, and that they can be enabled to make choices if given the opportunity.

Written and published by the Foundation for People with Learning Disabilities

£22.50 P&P 10%   ISBN: 0 901944 90 4   125pp

Choice Discovered

A training resource pack for frontline staff

Choice Discovered comprises of a video of participants in three Choice Initiative projects, and supporting written materials. It is aimed at frontline staff, volunteers, carers and advocates who support people with learning disabilities who have little or no speech. The written materials introduce participants to the key principles of communication and ways of discovering choices through exercises and discussion. The video illustrates many of the issues raised in the training pack, and is used as a starting point for discussion throughout the training. Topics explored include: methods of communication; the importance of building relationships; and creating more opportunities to communicate choice.

The pack can be used by anyone who has the confidence to run training courses – no special knowledge about communication is required.

Written and published by the Foundation for People with Learning Disabilities

£80.00 P&P 10%   Video running time: 18 mins   34pp

A Guide to Services for Adults with Autistic Spectrum Disorders for Commissioners and Providers

RITA JORDAN, GLENYS JONES AND HUGH MORGAN

The Care Standards Act and other policy changes including 'Best Value', will inevitably impact upon the quality and range of services that are commissioned for adults with an autistic spectrum disorder. Current estimates are that 500,000 people within the UK fall within the autistic spectrum, this is the largest identified single group of people falling under learning disability services that receive no individual recognition. This guide aims to provide guidance for the commissioner and service provider in developing and delivering innovative service models that really meet individual need rather than the traditional patterns of service delivery.

Written for professionals who commission or provide services for adults with an autistic spectrum disorder. It also offers valuable advice to care manager; practitioners; GPs; psychiatrists; psychologists; community nurses and social workers.

Published by the Foundation for People with Learning Disabilities

£12.50 P&P £1.80   ISBN: 1 903645 01 8   24pp

A Guide to Services for Children with Autistic Spectrum Disorders for Commissioners and Providers
RITA JORDAN, GLENYS JONES AND HUGH MORGAN

Autistic spectrum disorders involve developmental differences in social understanding and interaction, in all forms of communication and in flexible thinking and behaviour. Early diagnosis followed by effective early intervention for the child and family can make a real difference to the outcome. This publication serves a brief guide to autistic spectrum disorders and developments in education and social welfare. It aims to help agencies to provide a range of services to meet the needs of the individual child.

Written for professionals who commission in health, education or social services and provide services for children with an autistic spectrum disorder, it also offers valuable advice to care manager; practitioners; GPs; psychiatrists; psychologists; community nurses and social workers.

Published by the Foundation for People with Learning Disabilities

£16.00 P&P 10%   ISBN: 1 903645 01 8   24pp

Other resources available from the Foundation for People with Learning Disabilities

In addition to the publications listed here the Foundation for People with Learning Disabilities has a number of FREE information booklets and other resources. These can be downloaded from the following website www.learningdisabilities.org.uk